Work

P9-DEE-851

KEY CONCEPTS

Published

Barbara Adam, *Time*
Alan Aldridge, *Consumption*
Alan Aldridge, *The Market*
Jakob Arnoldi, *Risk*
Colin Barnes and Geof Mercer, *Disability*
Darin Barney, *The Network Society*
Mildred Blaxter, *Health 2nd edition*
Harriet Bradley, *Gender*
Harry Brighouse, *Justice*
Mónica Brito Vieira and David Runciman, *Representation*
Steve Bruce, *Fundamentalism 2nd edition*
Joan Busfield, *Mental Illness*
Margaret Canovan, *The People*
Alejandro Colás, *Empire*
Mary Daly, *Welfare*
Anthony Elliott, *Concepts of the Self 2nd edition*
Steve Fenton, *Ethnicity 2nd edition*
Katrin Flikschuh, *Freedom*
Michael Freeman, *Human Rights 2nd edition*
Russell Hardin, *Trust*
Geoffrey Ingham, *Capitalism*
Fred Inglis, *Culture*
Robert H. Jackson, *Sovereignty*
Jennifer Jackson Preece, *Minority Rights*
Gill Jones, *Youth*
Paul Kelly, *Liberalism*
Anne Mette Kjær, *Governance*
Ruth Lister, *Poverty*
Jon Mandle, *Global Justice*
Anthony Payne and Nicola Phillips, *Development*
Judith Phillips, *Care*
Michael Saward, *Democracy*
John Scott, *Power*
Anthony D. Smith, *Nationalism 2nd edition*
Steven Peter Vallas, *Work*
Stuart White, *Equality*

Work

A Critique

Steven Peter Vallas

polity

Copyright © Steven Peter Vallas 2012

The right of Steven Peter Vallas to be identified as Author of this Work has been asserted in accordance with the UK Copyright, Designs and Patents Act 1988.

First published in 2012 by Polity Press

Polity Press
65 Bridge Street
Cambridge CB2 1UR, UK

Polity Press
350 Main Street
Malden, MA 02148, USA

All rights reserved. Except for the quotation of short passages for the purpose of criticism and review, no part of this publication may be reproduced, stored in a retrieval system, or transmitted, in any form or by any means, electronic, mechanical, photocopying, recording or otherwise, without the prior permission of the publisher.

ISBN-13: 978-0-7456-4678-7
ISBN-13: 978-0-7456-4679-4(pb)

A catalogue record for this book is available from the British Library.

Typeset in 10.5 on 12 pt Sabon
by Servis Filmsetting Ltd, Stockport, Cheshire

The publisher has used its best endeavours to ensure that the URLs for external websites referred to in this book are correct and active at the time of going to press. However, the publisher has no responsibility for the websites and can make no guarantee that a site will remain live or that the content is or will remain appropriate.

Every effort has been made to trace all copyright holders, but if any have been inadvertently overlooked the publisher will be pleased to include any necessary credits in any subsequent reprint or edition.

For further information on Polity, visit our website:
www.politybooks.com

Contents

Figures and Tables

Figures

Tables

1

Introduction

Social scientists of widely varying persuasions – from Adam Smith, Karl Marx, and Max Weber to the Chicago School of sociology – have long acknowledged the centrality of work in all social and cultural life. They confronted the industrialization process, and were keenly aware of the ways in which industrial capitalism gripped the working lives of peasants, artisans, landowners, and merchants. As it did so, it remade the social landscape, refashioned the temporal rhythms of human experience, and redefined the way that authority, community, gender, and domestic life were all defined. Indeed, it might be said that classical social theory was one sustained debate over the division of labor modernity had wrought, and how it was likely to shape the character of human life.

What of our own era? How are the withering away of manufacturing industries, the spread of digital media, the rise of financial models of work and organizations, and the global mobility of production processes combining to transform our everyday working lives and identities? Has the wish for full-time employment in a stable career now become an exercise in nostalgia? Has a new, "post-Fordist," regime of work emerged, with instability and uncertainty constituting permanent features of the economic landscape? And which (if any) of these developments can be submitted to democratic choice rather than to the blind forces of the marketplace? To pose these questions is to acknowledge that long-established assumptions about the nature of work have been disrupted, and that the very concept of "work" now warrants close and careful deliberation.

Of course, there is no shortage of discussions about work. Yet in the USA, especially, managerial assumptions have proven so powerful as to sideline unsponsored inquiry into the forms that work is beginning to assume. Indeed, at their most extreme, managerial statements about work have become minor industries in their own right, as in the case of Peters and Waterman's *In Search of Excellence* (which has spun off multiple small businesses), Spencer Johnson's *Who Moved My Cheese?* (now available in a special edition for pre-teens), or Daniel Pink's *Free Agent Nation* (which invites its readers to regard themselves as their own CEOs). For their part, policy analysts often do address workplace issues, but commonly adhere to a formulaic montage of well-worn solutions. Should unemployment insurance benefits be extended? How will increases in the minimum wage affect the labor market? Dare we consider public works programs, or paid family leave? Unasked are questions about the forces that govern the structure of work organizations, why some jobs are valued so much more highly than others, how stereotypes of the most "appropriate" workers for a given occupation influence the distribution of opportunities at work, or whether work might begin to reflect the wishes of those who perform it. All too often, questions of agency and choice in the economic realm have been relegated to the personal advice columns in the business section, which unfailingly school their readers in how to compromise with one's boss. Images of muffled dissent and cynicism find expression in such outlets as *Dilbert* and *The Office*.

If discourse on work in the United States is a function of the political and ideological characteristics of US society, it should not surprise us that the market for workplace analysis displays a family resemblance to that which governs tabloid TV talk shows, rewarding writers who can make the most spectacular claims about the trends gripping our working lives. Hence we find Jeremy Rifkin (2004) declaring the "end of work," Stanley Aronowitz and William DiFazio (1995) alluding to the "jobless future," and Ulrich Beck (2000) holding forth on the collapse of the "work society." Such sensationalism is of course counterbalanced by careful and deliberate social scientific analyses of work. But these are usually sequestered within academic journals far removed from the public eye. Worse, perhaps, they are subject to a division of labor that carves work up into a welter of competing trades that enjoy little coordination. Thus sociology of work coexists uneasily alongside parallel literatures devoted to the study of organizations, occupations, labor markets, professions, and economic networks. Since each trade favors its own conceptual tools and jargon, little fruitful discussion ensues across the boundaries that demarcate each field.

In this book, I try to put at least some of the pieces back together. Three goals seem especially crucial here. One involves the labor of integration – that is, an effort to pull together, in a succinct and thoughtful manner, the disparate strands of thought that scholars have generated with respect to "work" in recent decades. A second objective involves the labor of critique – that is, to interrogate the main lines of scholarly work that have developed, in an effort to open up analytic paths that seem especially likely to advance the frontiers of the field. A third is to sketch out a view toward work that might spill over academic fields, engaging issues that ought to be on the agenda for public debate.

Approaching Work

Work is a primordial part of the human condition; like the biblical poor, it will always be with us. Yet the specific *form* that work assumes has varied enormously across historical periods and national boundaries. This is certainly the case today, as many of our conceptions of "work" have grown contested and ambiguous. We ought therefore to reflect on what the term "work" means, how that meaning has shifted in recent years, and why.

At the most abstract level, we can define work as *any expenditure of human effort aimed at producing a socially valued good or service*. This is a deceptively simple definition, however, and one that requires several provisos. First, few workers get to choose the institutional system in which their labor will be expended. Rather, we must typically conform to the dominant institutional structures that define how work must be performed. A related point is that the institutional structure that is most familiar to us – work as paid employment, performed in exchange for a wage or salary – is only one of several types that have developed over time. Indeed, the dominance of wage-labor in relation to the labor market is a recent construct, and one whose triumph often required the exercise of cultural and political power, and even military force.

Moreover, although we have come to view paid employment as the only "real" form of work, in fact work has been defined entirely outside of the labor market for the great bulk of human history. This is certainly the case with *unfree* or "forced" labor – slavery, serfdom, prison labor, child labor, and other forms of servitude – which persists in many societies (including our own) to this day.[1] An equally important form of non-market labor is that of domestic or household work, performed in order to reproduce one's daily life. Farming communities that provided their own food, clothing, and other material goods had little need for any labor market; family members were expected to shoulder the daily tasks required to eke out a living from the land, producing goods for sale only at the margins of their daily lives. More familiar to us are the many forms of work required in our own families, in the form of cooking, washing, cleaning, and caring for young children – certainly, work by any definition.

So dominant has the labor market become in our own society that we have come to view paid employment, or wage labor, as the only "real" form of work. This would have struck our predecessors as a most unusual point of view. As the American historian Jacqueline Dowd Hall (2000) reports, when cotton mills first began to appear in the American South, farming families often referred to factory work as "public work." They viewed work outside the bounds of one's farm as a strange phenomenon – one that engulfed unfortunates who had lost their land to the banks, and had few alternatives but to enter the labor market. Moreover, for much of the nineteenth century, protest against wage labor – operating with the notion of the independent artisan who owned "his own competence" – construed it in terms of "wage slavery." How much has changed.

And change continues to happen, for paid employment is not a static thing. The boundary between work in this sense and "non-work" has become an increasingly difficult line to draw in recent years. This is obviously the case for professional or sales employees tethered to their jobs by their trusty smartphones and portable PCs: here the boundary between the job and private life begins to break down (Fraser 2002; Orlikowski 2007). It is also the case in a growing number of ambiguous situations, such as those that are familiar to graduate students, participants in workfare programs, and, increasingly, to unpaid interns as well. Indeed, graduate students have begun to assume so many teaching obligations that they have sometimes sought to form unions as a matter of self-defense, only to have courts deny them legal status as workers (they have ruled that graduate students are not workers, but students in professional training programs). For their part, workfare participants often seem to be half workers and half public wards. Like workers, they must be paid in accordance with minimum wage laws, and are protected under sexual harassment laws. But, like public wards, they cannot choose their own place of employment, and cannot form unions to defend themselves (see Krinsky 2007). And many employers, it seems, are happy to arrange internships in lieu of paid employment – a point the US Department of Labor has begun to explore (Perlin 2011). In cases such as these, the very definition of work is contested, involving litigation and judicial rulings to decide whether incumbents of these roles are protected under US labor law.

A final point follows from the above. Whether an activity warrants the term "work" even by our narrow, market, standards is not simply a function of the activities it entails. For the very same functions may or may not be "work," depending on the social and organizational context in which the activity occurs. The very same activity – say, listening to someone's emotional problems, driving a car, or having sex – means very different things, and involves very different experiences, depending on whether the activity is performed by a worker engaged for pay or someone in a social (or non-market) relationship. Indeed, one of the defining features of contemporary capitalist societies is that it is very difficult to imagine any activity that *cannot* be performed in a market context, for pay.

This book will largely be concerned with work in the form of paid employment. It is written from the standpoint of what may be one of the more peculiar occupations one can imagine, yet one that its practitioners find inspiring: that of the sociologist *of* work. For our job is that of explaining why work itself is defined in certain ways; why jobs are allocated to the members of some groups and not to others; how the structure of work and employment is evolving in an era of global capitalism, and how these shifts are likely to affect both our social structure and our own personal lives. You might view this book as something of a user's guide or manual for this most peculiar trade.

Three Rules of Thumb

Any trade will of course need some basic principles, or axioms, that can guide practitioners as they set about doing their work. Of course, as with any area in the social sciences, the sociology of work is often riddled with sharp divisions and debates (these are discussed later in this chapter). In spite of these divisions – or, perhaps, as the outcome of them – sociologists interested in work as a social construct have hammered out three rough principles that do provide coherence for the field. The first is the simple yet profound argument that work is *consequential* for human life, both individually and collectively. Second, and equally important, is the axiom that work cannot be viewed as a mere economic transaction, or as the outcome of technological imperatives; rather, work is almost always embedded in social and institutional settings that lend it a different character than a purely economic approach can reveal. A third point is that what actually happens at work often departs, in subtle yet vital ways, from the formal rules and official policies inscribed within employee handbooks. There is a hidden underside of workplace life, often invisible to authority figures, where informal norms and practices are established that often stand at odds with formal expectations.

The primacy of production

Although the most celebrated theorist who embraced the "primacy of production" thesis is surely Karl Marx, in truth the modern origins of the idea can be traced to John Locke and other Enlightenment thinkers who developed the philosophical notion of *homo faber*, or a conception of human nature that distinguishes the human species on the basis of our capacity to create, or to use tools and concepts with which to transform the natural world. Indeed, in this view, humans are doubly creative: we not only transform the external world through our labor; in so doing, we also transform ourselves. It is in this sense that work constitutes an especially formative influence at both the individual and the collective levels of analysis.

This view has been widely embraced in the sociological literature on work. Literature on the relation between work and the self abounds. E. C. Hughes, a major figure within the Chicago School of sociology, argued that "a man's work [sic] is one of the more important parts of his social identity, of his self; indeed of his fate in the one life he has to live." Work, from this point of view, is "one of the things by which he is judged, and certainly one of the more significant things by which he judges himself" (1994 [1951: 57]). Much evidence attests to the validity of Hughes's point. Examining existing studies of the mentalities that accompany particular occupational domains, Bensman and Lilienfield (1991: xv) found occupationally specific "attitudes towards everyday life," and viewed these as the outcome of "habits of thought that emerge and are developed in the practice of an occupation, profession, or craft." In a series of studies conducted over the span of several decades, Melvyn Kohn and his colleagues (1969, 2006; Kohn and Schooler 1983) repeatedly found that the occupational conditions under which people are employed (for example, whether the design of their jobs gives them a bit of autonomy or freedom from close supervision) have enduring effects on their psychological functioning, shaping people's levels of intellectual flexibility, self-esteem, and even parental values. Myriad studies have found strong connections between aspects of the work situation and such mental health outcomes as psychological distress, depression, or hostility (see Kornhauser 1965; Karasek 1979, 1981). Physical health too is affected by the nature of one's work. A recent French study (Cambois 2004) found that after controlling for relevant variables, white-collar men who were promoted tended to live significantly longer lives than did their counterparts who were left behind. The general implication of this literature is simple: the job shapes the person to a substantial extent.

But the structure of work does more than this. How work is arranged also has massive institutional and cultural effects that are evident at the collective level of analysis. As E. P. Thompson's landmark studies showed (1964), the coming of industrial capitalism brought about unprecedented conceptions of time and work discipline, reshaping the very sinews of everyday life during the eighteenth and nineteenth centuries. The stability or instability established by work institutions can have widespread effects on social control over whole populations. The absence of work for large segments of the population – whether during the Great Depression, or within poor or ghetto communities today – can have massive consequences, sometimes engendering large-scale movements to demand social change (Piven and Cloward 1977), and at other times straining the community's ability to exercise control over their own neighborhoods (Wilson 1996). Indeed, the economic historian Sebastian de Grazia (1994) was so struck by the weight industrial capitalism placed upon productive employment that he characterized the modern West as constituting a "work society." Ulrich Beck (2000: 63) believes that as Western societies have grown more secular, people have "lost their faith in God," and come to believe instead "in the godlike powers of work to provide everything sacred to them: prosperity, social position, personality [and] meaning in life."

To be sure, there are reasons to question such sweeping claims. The growing consumption of cultural goods, the proliferation of mass and digital media, and shifts in assumptions about the stability and longevity of attachments to any given firm have emboldened some theorists to challenge arguments concerning the salience of work and to question the presumed link between work and identity. In this latter view, identity is no longer so firmly anchored in the realm of production as in the past; rather, people increasingly define themselves by embracing one or another style of life, as reflected in their cultural tastes, style of dress, bodily comportment, speech, and personal style. In some accounts, the world of production has been overwhelmed or even invaded by cultural influences that stem from television, magazines, movies, and consumer goods. The relation between work and self thus becomes more complex or weakened, as regimes of personhood emerge that are more firmly rooted in the nation-state, consumer markets, and ideologies of citizenship than in the realm of production as such (Rose 1990).

Evaluating these claims, Leidner (2004) finds them to be narrowly one-sided and overdrawn, citing several considerations. Although one can certainly point to trends that have increased the importance of "non-work" influences in the production and presentation of self, there have also been countervailing trends that operate in the opposite direction. For one thing, the urge to consume often reinforces the need to work; and, indeed, the evidence suggests that American workers now labor substantially longer than was the case two or three decades ago. Although this trend has developed unevenly across different classes and groups (Hochschild 2001; Jacobs and Gerson 2004), the spread of 24/7 work schedules has increasingly impinged on the rhythms of family relations and cultural life more generally. A related development has been the dramatic increase in the proportion of adult women – especially those who are married and have young children – who have entered into the paid labor force, for this structural shift exposes a much larger swath of adults to the demands of work organizations than was true of previous generations. The expansion of professional and managerial occupations, which often fill jobs through national searches, has dispersed employees geographically, weakening extended family relations, and in turn actually reinforcing the growth of care work provided through the marketplace. Moreover, the rise of "knowledge work," especially among high-pressure professionals in technology-intensive industries, exposes workers to jobs that make increasingly demanding claims on their time and their souls; the concept of the "greedy institution" seems if anything more applicable than ever before (Kunda 1992; Ross 2008; Kunda and Ailon-Souday 2005; Sennett

1999). And analysts studying new "high-performance" work organization or systems using Total Quality Management have often alleged that these structures seek to incorporate workers' identities to a much greater extent than under work informed by older, more traditionally bureaucratic patterns.

Nor are the expansive demands of work on identity limited to professional and managerial work. As revealed in the literature on interactive service work, which by its very nature requires social interaction between the customer and the worker, employers increasingly seek to define, direct, and control the feelings and emotions that workers display while engaging in their jobs. These practices – immortalized by Hochschild (1983) in her study of the "emotional labor" performed by airline attendants at Delta Airlines – have the effect of enabling firms to lay claim to a broader proportion of workers' selves than was previously the case. Our emotional expressions and displays of internal feelings, which have long been a private, spontaneous part of social interaction, thus no longer belong to us, but become part of the very "product" that companies seek to put up for sale. Leidner (1993) finds reason to suggest that corporate efforts to standardize and control the worker's presentation of self can have potentially corrosive effects on our identities, fostering a cynicism and distanced relation toward others and toward one's self. In the line of these counter-tendencies, it seems safe to conclude that work continues to leave its mark on social life, though the nature of this link has changed in ways that warrant close and careful research.

Work as a social construct

Beginning in the 1970s, when the USA began to de-regulate industry after industry, economic institutions have increasingly been governed by what has come to be called "neo-liberalism" – the doctrine that not only economic institutions but whole societies operate most effectively when their resources are allocated in accordance with a purely market-driven logic, without resort to public or government intervention of any sort (see Harvey 2005, and chapter 6 below). This doctrine, which was actively encouraged by the Thatcher and Reagan governments, has been embraced by such powerful international lending agencies as the International Monetary Fund and the World Bank, vaulting neo-liberal thinking into the status of an unquestioned economic orthodoxy. This view often yields a starkly Darwinian assumption about economic institutions: Companies that adopt the most efficient organizational practices will thrive; those that do not will stagnate and die. From this point of view, the key forces driving the structure of work are the imperatives of the marketplace and the efficiency with which technology and other resources are used. Influences that stand at odds with efficiency considerations (including such biases as racism and sexism) are viewed as factors that impede the efficiency of work organizations. As such, they are projected to wilt and wither away as market competition selects them for extinction.

In the sociological view, arguments such as this – which are premised on the efficacy and "natural" character of the market – rest almost entirely on myth. This point can best be developed in relation to the views of Adam Smith, whose *Wealth of Nations* serves as the Bible of economic orthodoxy. Smith was one of a generation of thinkers who sought to pursue the development of institutional mechanisms that could hold in check the religious and ethnic wars that had plagued Western Europe during so much of the early modern period. Smith believed that the pursuit of economic advantage, through commerce and trade, had the advantage of binding nations together in the pursuit of rational lines of action, rather than the unbridled and often violent passions that religion had unleashed. Smith's analysis rested on two fundamental precepts. First, he argued that the general interest was, ironically, best served through the pursuit of individual gain. Because unbridled competition, if left to its own devices, allocated resources in accordance with the "invisible hand" of the marketplace, the results would be more rational and effective than any government body could possibly achieve. And, second, Smith argued that the rise of market economies was inevitable, for it reflected the "consequence of a certain propensity in human nature . . . to truck, barter, and exchange one thing for another."

Smith's argument has if anything gained increasing relevance in the two and a half centuries since it was developed.

It continues to find contemporary application, even in popular culture (think of such figures as Gordon Gekko in the famous film *Wall Street*). Perhaps the single most powerful response to Smith's perspective, and to the myth of the marketplace generally, was developed by the eminent economic anthropologist Karl Polanyi (1944), whose work warrants close consideration.

In *The Great Transformation*, Polanyi made two interrelated points. First, he argued that, in fact, the great majority of human cultures – including Western culture until a little over a century ago – have organized work on the basis of custom and tradition rather than any impulse to pursue individual gain. Indeed, the production and exchange of goods have been so deeply embedded within social and cultural institutions that pre-industrial societies did not actually *have* "economies" that were structurally distinct from kinship or village institutions. To project currently dominant market norms backward onto human history – as Smith does when he roots the "propensity to truck and barter" within human nature – thus does violence to the actual history of economic institutions.

Second, Polanyi contended that the very notion of a "self-regulating market" is itself highly deceptive. For one thing, the triumph of markets itself rested on political force (often, the stripping away of rights and resources enjoyed by a large sector of the laboring population). Moreover, markets cannot long endure without political and legal regulation, for by their very nature market forces engender instability, uncertainty, and even chaos. (If the point needs emphasis, the economic crises that began in 2008 make the point reasonably well.) Indeed, government supports, inducements, and subsidies of all sorts are typically needed to sustain the ongoing success of the market – success that is (ironically enough) then celebrated by the advocates of the "self-regulating market." The point here is that purely economic approaches toward work offer only partial, misleading, or reductionist perspectives, for they tend to distort a complex social and political reality. Work and economic institutions, in other words, are social constructs that cannot be reduced to market forces and efficiency considerations alone.

This same point has repeatedly emerged from the very

beginning of sociologically informed analysis of work. Until the 1930s, management thinking generally operated on the basis of *homo economicus* – "economic man" (to use the gendered dialect). In this view, workers are rationally acting individuals who respond to material rewards. This approach provided the point of departure for one of the most famous research projects in this field – the Hawthorne studies, conducted at AT&T's manufacturing plant at Hawthorne, Illinois. The team of researchers was led by Elton Mayo, a Harvard psychologist who designed a series of studies at the company's Western Electric facility (see Roethlisberger and Dickson 1939). These studies have generated too much discussion and debate to be reiterated here. Two points must suffice in this context. The first concerns the basic findings that emerged from Mayo's research: even when workers were presented with significant material incentives for increasing their pace of work, they typically refused, preferring to forgo significant sums of bonus pay. The reason is that workers did not behave simply as individuals seeking monetary rewards. Rather, they acted in accordance with the norms and codes of behavior established in their work groups, which overrode – and sometimes punished – self-seeking behavior.

A second point stems from the Hawthorne researchers' interpretation, which held that sharply distinct logics seemed to govern the behavior of the people in the Hawthorne plant. The actions of managers and executives were informed by the "logic of efficiency," which resembled the notion of economic man. This was a normative orientation that motivated managers on the basis of incentives, bonuses, and individual gain. Yet, alongside this logic, there existed a second, more collectively oriented normative system, which the authors called a "logic of sentiments." This orientation invited workers to adhere to the norms of their work group, and to derive a sense of belonging and recognition that such solidarity could provide. Essentially, the Hawthorne researchers criticized management for naively projecting their own market ethos onto workers – a narcissistic posture that tended to foster enmity and antagonism within the firm, rather than the motivation that companies seek.

The Hawthorne studies had broad implications for the study of work. First, the authors opened up a more reflexive, self-aware approach toward the study of industrial work. Second, these studies led to careful analysis of the research of work groups as a determinant of industrial attitudes and behavior. And, third, they opened up what would become the human relations school of thought – an influential approach that stresses the informal codes of behavior and communication that companies adopt. Perhaps the most important consequence – since reiterated in dozens of studies – has been the recognition that the social organization of work is often governed by social, cultural, and political influences that have little or nothing to do with the pursuit of efficiency.

Two important strands of thought have followed from this last point. One focuses on the internal dynamics that shape workplace behavior. Here, ethnographic case studies have explored the social forces that influence how work is defined, how technologies are selected, and how production processes take shape. One of the most revealing studies in this vein is Robert Thomas's *What Machines Can't Do* (1994). A sociologist at MIT, Thomas conducted a series of case studies in four different manufacturing settings, posing the following types of questions. What seems to drive the organizational and technological innovations that unfold in these industries? Who proposes and designs new technologies for production, and how are these innovations introduced? Thomas's studies had the advantage of moving the analysis backward in time – that is, reconstructing the processes through which innovations were first proposed, well before they were actually introduced. They also moved the analysis downward in the firm, encompassing rank-and-file workers who confronted new production processes on the shop floor itself.

In most of the contexts Thomas studied, engineers played a critical role. Yet there was a key difference that rankled many engineers: the division between *product* engineers (who were often employed at headquarters, in tandem with top executives), and *industrial* or process engineers (who were often employed at manufacturing facilities out in the field). The former group enjoyed great prestige, autonomy, and resources, while members of the latter group were defined as little more than industrial grunts. Product engineers often generated new designs with little regard for the manufacturing process, while industrial engineers were defined as the "over the wall guys" – that is, they were simply expected to conform to the product specifications they received from the product engineers. This arrangement often produced a sharp sense of deprivation among industrial engineers. Consequently, they and their managers often looked for ways to enhance their occupation's status and autonomy within the firm. Such interests often found expression in the form of proposals for new production processes – new technologies that employed robotics, or computer-integrated manufacturing systems, or automated systems for the storage and retrieval of parts.

In proposing these kinds of innovations, engineers and their managers typically emphasized the gains the company would enjoy with respect to its return on investment (ROI). Yet, in fact, such gains often proved illusory. In most of the cases Thomas examined, the promised improvements in ROI never materialized. Indeed, top executives seldom bothered to scrutinize the actual outcomes of projects or to evaluate their success in meeting the projected gains. One of the few constants Thomas found was that leadership of a major project did indeed enhance the career of the manager or lead engineer who proposed it – though it produced little structural change in the position of the industrial engineers within the firm. Efficiency served as a rationale, then, masking efforts by occupational groups seeking to advance their own power and prestige. As Thomas puts it, "the rules of the corporate game required that all participants present themselves as rational, calculating utility maximizers, but beneath the official rules an entirely different game was being played."

The hidden underside of work

Many of the richest and most revealing studies in the sociology of work have been conducted in manufacturing settings, where analysts have consistently unearthed patterns of covert defiance, subterfuge, and restriction of output despite the most determined efforts by management to exercise full control over the efforts of employees. One of the lessons that emerges from this literature is that even the most subordinate-level workers, exposed to the most stringent forms of control, can find ways of neutralizing, disrupting, or renegotiating managerial regimes to their own advantage.

This was certainly the case in the early studies by Duke sociologist Donald Roy (1952, 1954, 1960). Roy was a doctoral student at the University of Chicago who had substantial industrial experience. Conducting participant observation as a machine-tool operative at a South Side Chicago metalworking plant, Roy found that workers invested a substantial proportion of their creative energies in the ongoing effort to outwit management and sidestep its policies. Although their employer established strict rules and an onerous system of piece-rate payment, Roy's co-workers used alliances with support personnel, go-slow production techniques, and creative uses of the time clock as elements of a general strategy that enabled them to garner levels of pay and autonomy that management fervently wished to deny them. As Roy puts it, "operators and their allies joined forces in certain situations in a manner not only unmistakably at variance with the carefully prepared designs of staff experts but even in flagrant violation of strongly held managerial "moral principles of shop floor behavior" (1954: 256). David Halle (1984), studying a New Jersey petrochemical refinery, likewise found that blue-collar workers often performed their jobs in a manner that bore little resemblance to the recipes and practices the company printed. Because these workers engaged in close contact with systems and equipment over long stretches of time, they were able to accumulate knowledge about the quirks of the production process that were found in no formal documents and that could not be deduced from formal scientific expertise. Such practical knowledge gave these workers substantial power over the method and pace of their work, and gave them an important measure of independence from their managers. It also gave them a vital stake in keeping the depth and even the very existence of their hidden knowledge largely to themselves. In a similar vein, my own research on pulp and paper manufacturing plants in the US South revealed that when manual workers encountered machine superintendents who showed insufficient respect for the workers' knowledge and dignity, what transpired were "authority contests" in which workers sought to teach their supervisors important lessons about reciprocity and respect. Machines would run "in the ditch" for whole shifts as workers sought to modify their supervisors' behavior, or, if necessary, to inflict mortal injuries on their supervisors' careers (Vallas 2003a, 2006).

Yet the hidden underside of workplace life is hardly restricted to manufacturing settings; virtually all workplaces have "backstage" regions where outsiders are not allowed. Technical support personnel answering phone calls from troubled users, for example, often cope with their jobs by finding novel uses of the chat-room technologies at their disposal. Instead of using them merely to query other workers about specific problems customers report, they often use them to share derisive jokes and stories about the ignorant customers they have on the line. Restaurant cooks and food servers often develop tricks, ways of cutting corners, and imaginative ways of handling food that must by their very nature not migrate beyond the kitchen door (Fine 1996). And ill-behaved customers may at times risk having hot soup "inadvertently" dumped in their laps (Paules 1991). Put simply, the informal culture that develops among routine workers often stands at odds with formal rules and expectations, with effects on the firm's operations that can take any of several forms.

For example, cultural anthropologist Julian Orr (1996) studied photocopy-repair technicians employed by Xerox. Although, on the surface, this seems be a relatively isolating and unrewarding job, Orr's research unearthed a rich occupational community. Workers commonly socialized in their off hours, sharing not only meals and drinks but also an unending supply of "war stories" – tales of their encounters with especially difficult models of machines. This was not idle talk; participation in these communal activities was in fact vital to the worker's ability to do the job. Workers resisted company efforts to codify their knowledge, preferring to keep it in the form of their own "community of practice." Here, the informal culture of work actually seemed to aid the company in its operations (though managers often failed to recognize this fact).

Jeffrey Sallaz uncovered a layered set of games – some obvious and authorized, others hidden and unauthorized – in his study of Las Vegas gambling casinos (2002, 2009). Sallaz, a sociologist at the University of Arizona, gained certification as a blackjack dealer and went to work at a large casino on the strip. There he encountered as tightly controlled a managerial regime as one can imagine – this casino used video-surveillance to identify cheaters or card counters, and established strict rules governing interactions between blackjack dealers and players. Yet, even under these circumstances, Sallaz's co-workers taught him an elaborate repertoire of unofficial tricks that tilted the game to their own advantage. Dealers found ways to help generous tippers win at blackjack more frequently; they tilted the game in the opposite direction when confronted with deadbeats who tipped poorly if at all. Here, the very outcome of a strictly policed game could still be influenced by the informal tactics the dealers had learned.

A final illustration of the role that informal culture plays can be found in John Weeks's 2004 study of a British bank ("BritArm"). Two features of this workplace seem especially interesting. First, clerical and administrative staff at this firm had developed a keen awareness of the concept of organizational culture – so much so that Weeks calls them "lay ethnographers" (see also Kunda 1992). Second, they used their conceptual sophistication to subject the firm to an unrelentingly critical analysis, establishing a "culture of complaint" that was predicated on what they saw as the chronic failure of the firm to achieve the standards of excellence that commonly circulate in the business press. Although this culture seems to subvert the organization's goals, Weeks concludes that it in fact provided a much-needed source of solidarity and cohesion among the employees' ranks, without which BritArm might not have functioned nearly as well as it did.

It is important to point out that the capacity of any occupational group to evade managerial direction is by no means a constant. It depends on a host of institutional and cultural factors, including the strength of workers' ties to one another, the demographic make-up of the occupation, the levels of skill that workers command, the spatial layout of the workplace, and the managerial treatment workers experience at work. The factors that impinge on worker resistance are nowhere better catalogued than in the study by Randy Hodson (2001). Based on careful coding of ethnographic studies of workplace life, Hodson was able to conduct a sophisticated analysis of the factors accounting for worker resistance to managerial expectations. He found that resistance was especially strong in workplaces where bosses subjected workers to harsh and abusive treatment, or failed to act in ways that seemed competent or worthy of workers' respect. Hodson also found that professional employees were the least likely to engage in resistance – and that highly skilled manual workers were consistently the most likely to challenge the boss. Less skilled workers, and those employed in workplaces where turnover rates were high, were less inclined or less capable of challenging managerial practices. Still, evidence suggests that it is by no means safe to assume that formal rules and expectations are the only relevant guide to workplace practices. This very assumption has short-circuited the careers of many aspiring managers.

Schools of Thought in the Sociology of Work

It is one thing to sketch out the general coordinates and principles that sociologists of work tend to share. It is quite another to unpack the divisions that arise among our ranks – divisions often drawn on the basis of divergent theoretical perspectives. On what basis do analysts formulate concrete lines of analysis – that is, their research questions and problems for study? What are the dominant schools of thought in the field today, and what assumptions does each make? In the remainder of this chapter, I briefly address these questions, limiting the discussion to contemporary schools of thought.

The key schools of thought can be seen as four: Marxist, interactionist, feminist, and institutionalist approaches. There are, of course, points of overlap, and these four by no means exhaust the varieties of sociological thinking on this terrain.[2] We do well to grasp the distinctive nature of each point of view.

Marxist theories of work

The key to Marx's own analysis of labor – and to that of the generations of thinkers who have followed in his tracks – is his analysis of commodity production. Capitalism can, after all, be defined as a system that is based on generalized commodity production. Under capitalism, goods and services can only be produced with an eye toward the expansion of the value they contain. Indeed, as capitalism develops, it becomes less and less important what a given company actually produces; what matters is whether its commodities can be exchanged for more money than they cost to produce. Then of course the money can be reinvested in more commodities, engendering a cycle of purchase, production, sale, and further purchases, resulting in an accumulation of capital on an ever-expanding basis.

What is unique to Marxist theory is its emphasis on the peculiar results that occur when labor time itself becomes a commodity that is routinely bought and sold. Workers sell their labor time on the market, of course; they have little choice, since this is the only means of subsistence they possess. Yet what is important here is that, after selling this commodity, workers remain in possession of it even as the new owner – the employer – sets about using it to the fullest extent possible. What ensues is an ongoing struggle, which first appeared in small workshops and now reverberates in workplaces throughout the globe: *workers* seek to limit the exploitation of their own labor (sometimes having to safeguard life and limb), while *employers* respond in kind, mobilizing every effort imaginable to exercise control over the labor time they nominally own. And, as capitalism expands, a larger and larger proportion of any society's labor force is drawn into the logic of commodity production, with results that begin to reverberate on the political stage.

Marx himself, writing at the transition to industrial capitalism, emphasized the varied forms that coercion assumed at the point of production itself. The actual mechanisms utilized varied widely. At times, it was the onerous role of the overseer, armed with economic penalties (the "whip of hunger") that occupied center-stage. Elsewhere, the function of control passed over into the machinery, which itself dominated the worker's motions. At all points during the rise of industrial capitalism, intense battles were fought over the length of the working day, the use of child labor, and the rights of workers to organize on their own behalf. Under contemporary capitalism, several new forms of control have appeared (some of which are discussed in the next chapter). Such historical variations aside, at least three points are common properties of Marxist analyses of work. First, analysts view the sphere of production as an especially determinative institutional nexus, not least because it conditions the distribution of power within the society as a whole. Second, the assumption is that the wage-labor relationship is by nature inherently conflictual or antagonistic. Thus any adequate analysis must proceed by examining how power and control are exercised over labor (and how workers actively resist). A third and related point is that the capitalist division of labor is marked not only by the enduring enmity between capital and labor, but also between mental and manual labor. Although at the outset "the labor process unites the labor of the head with that of the hand," the development of capitalism sunders this bond: "Later on, they part company, and even become deadly foes" (Marx 1967 [1865]).

Marxist theory has proven to be one of the most fertile of all approaches toward work. For this reason, much of chapter 2 is devoted to what has come to be called labor-process theory, a perspective that has been partly inspired by Marxist analysis, and that has driven a substantial proportion of empirical research and theoretical debate. Though this perspective has come under strong criticism in recent decades, it warrants sustained consideration.

The interactionist perspective

The "symbolic interactionist" perspective, a uniquely American product, was a critical feature of the Chicago School of sociology at the beginning of the twentieth century. One of its focal concerns centered on the social ecology of human settlement in Chicago's bustling urban environment. These ecological concerns led to a highly distinctive, influential, and internally diverse approach toward the study of work and occupations. In this view, the division of labor and the occupational structure that emerges are the culmination of ongoing processes of negotiation, as the members of different occupational groups seek to affix meanings to their work and to derive a sense of identity from their occupational position. This suggests that the division of labor, and the occupational categories that emerge in any society, are inevitably bound up with the exercise of power and with the ability to identify critical moral problems that occupational specialists are equipped to address. The management of these moral problems, and the mobilization of occupational claims, are viewed as the grounds on which occupational privilege often rests.

These themes were first established by Everett C. Hughes, a leading exponent of the interactionist approach toward work, and a figure whose students included such luminaries as Anselm Strauss, Howard Becker, Blanche Geer, Eliot Freidson, and Erving Goffman. Hughes's own writings exerted obvious influence on these scholars. For Hughes, the most important aspect of the division of labor was its division of work and workers into two broad sets of occupations – the humble and the proud. The latter, represented by the professions, succeeded in gaining a "license" (or socially established right) to perform highly specialized tasks, gaining this by eliciting a broad "mandate" (or broad public support) affirming that they, and they alone, have the training and sensibilities to perform a given type of work. Hughes takes pains to note that although professionals claim merely to solve already existing problems, in truth, members of the professions quite often actively *define* the very nature of those problems, and in so doing exercise considerable authority over social life. Their ability to do this is predicated on the ability of professionals to define their work as distinctly different from (and often, as morally superior to) more humble pursuits. Yet a key part of Hughes's analysis suggests that even such "noble" occupational pursuits manifest precisely the same features as do humble occupations, including the performance of "dirty" work, deceptive activities, and unethical practices of various sorts, all of which must be hidden from public view. Demonstrating this fact was indeed one of the goals that led Hughes to focus particular attention on humble occupations: since these workers often lack the resources with which to hide the secrets of their trade, or to block the access of the researcher, the features that are shared by "proud" and "humble" occupations alike can more easily be glimpsed. This is why he wrote (using gendered language) that:

[W]e need to rid ourselves of any concepts which keep us from seeing that the essential problems of men at work are the same, whether they do their work in the laboratories of some famous institution or in the messiest vat room of a pickle factory. Until we can find a point of view and concepts which will enable us to make comparisons between the junk peddler and the professor without intent to debunk the one and patronize the other, we cannot do our best work in this field. (1994 [1951]: 61)

As an example of his effort to unearth the universal features of "men at work," Hughes discusses the work situation of the jazz musician – certainly, a suspect occupation in 1950s Chicago. He finds that the jazz artist is often loathe to submit his or her work to the judgment of lay audiences, for then "they are getting too close – they are impinging on his private world too much" – and, accordingly, the musician will use a variety of means with which to distance the performers from their audiences. "This is a problem not only among musicians, but in teaching, medicine, dentistry, the arts, and many other fields. It is a chronic source of ego-wound and possibly of antagonism" (ibid. 65). Hughes's insights were later developed in classic works by Becker (1963).

Hughes's writings provided much of the impetus for the sociology of professions (see, especially, Abbott 1988), and gave rise to a perspective known as "negotiated order" theory, which has been applied in hospitals, mental institutions, police organizations, and many other settings. Gary Alan Fine's rich and insightful study, *Kitchens: The Culture of Restaurant Work* (1996), stands as a case in point. Immersing himself in the operations of four different mid-price restaurants, Fine sought to understand how cooks actively respond to the structural constraints they confront at work. To keep restaurants afloat, cooks must fashion what Fine calls a "commonwealth of cuisine" – rich subcultures that help to ensure that tolerable work relations emerge in these settings, and that food is produced well enough to satisfy the needs of the most important audiences involved – managers, customers, food servers, and the cooks themselves. Indeed, one of the points that emerges in Fine's study is that "all art is work, and all work is art" – by which the author reminds us of the aesthetic aspects of the work that people do, which they strive hard to protect even in the face of seemingly overwhelming practical, commercial, and organizational demands.

The interactionist perspective has made numerous contributions to the sociology of work. It is particularly well suited to uncover the hidden underside of work in particular situations, and the informal processes through which power and authority are negotiated within concrete work situations (Strauss 1978; Fine 1984). If the Chicago perspective has been partly eclipsed by other approaches, it continues to inform important research on workplace culture, the coping strategies workers develop at work, and the relation between work and the self. Yet its very strengths – its emphasis on the construction of meanings at work, on the importance of occupationally based identities, and on the active negotiation of workplace boundaries – produce certain vulnerabilities. Critics have rightly pointed to the inattention to social structure that is evident in some applications of this perspective. Likewise, the point can be made that by pursuing the *common* features of all occupational life – "the essential problems of all men at work" – interactionists tend to flatten out the *differences* that are built into the structure and the experience of work.

Feminist theories of work

It is by now well known that the US military struggle against fascism during World War II depended crucially on the labor of women in thousands of factories producing aircraft, tanks, and munitions. Yet, when the war was over, women workers encountered a deeply rooted social and political campaign to return them to the private sphere, one of unpaid work in the home (Milkman 1987). Faced with little prospect of staking out an enduring claim to paid employment, and with a slack labor market weakening demand for labor generally, many working- and middle-class women had little choice but to wax domestic – at least in the short term. In the longer term, however, the US war effort set in motion larger processes that have widely disrupted long-standing assumptions about the "natural" order of things with respect to work and occupational life – that is to say, about the "place" of women and men within the sphere of paid employment.

These changes are often described as revolutionary – and it is easy to see why. Although women have *always* worked – few families could afford otherwise – by the turn of the nineteenth century, the separation of paid employment from the home had located women's "place" within the home – or, for single women, in routine office work, or in service and cleaning work (as for immigrants and minority women). All this was dramatically challenged during the second half of the twentieth century: women's rates of labor-force participation rose dramatically, nearly converging with men's rates. The educational attainment of women matched and in some cases transcended that of men. Where women had previously been excluded from highly privileged occupational terrain such as the law, engineering, management, and medicine, women now successfully struggled for admission into these domains. The law acknowledged and protected these changes, banning discrimination on the basis of sex.

All these changes have widely and powerfully acted to disrupt long-standing conceptions of gender and work. Yet they have done so in highly uneven ways. Although occupational segregation by sex has undeniably declined, such changes are by no means consistently found across all occupations. Gender inequality in pay has proved remarkably persistent, even when we hold constant a variety of labor-market conditions. And many occupations have actually tended to grow more heavily feminized over time. Many theorists have begun to speak of a "stalled revolution," of partial and highly selective gains, and of deeply institutionalized inequalities that have by no means been sufficiently addressed. The picture looks even more sobering when one looks at the global division of labor: much of the factory work that is performed in the highly labor-intensive industries of the developing world is performed by women laboring under brutal circumstances. And many of the occupational gains that women have won in the developed world have had uneven effects on poor women in the developing world, who are often compelled to leave their own children while caring for the homes and children of affluent families in the advanced capitalist world (Hondagneu-Sotelo 2001; Ehrenreich and Hochschild 2003).

Mindful of these uneven and highly contradictory trends,

feminist scholars have given rise to an outpouring of probing, critical analysis of how gender shapes the nature of the work that people do and the meanings work holds in the eyes of those who perform it. What, for instance, actually *counts* as "work?" Why has the distinction between "men's" and "women's" work – that is, occupational segregation by sex – been so resilient even in the face of laws designed to uproot it? What social mechanisms explain why women remain severely underrepresented at the most powerful echelons of the corporate economy? And why are men and women generally paid so differentially, even when job-relevant factors are taken into account?

In posing these and other questions, feminist scholars have advanced a set of arguments that in some respects resemble those advanced by Marxist theorists. Where Marxist theorists emphasize the division between mental and manual labor, and thus the existence of powerful class inequalities at work, feminist theorists stress the *sexual* division of labor and the inequality that has historically unfolded between men and women at work. At issue is the deeply embedded tendency to define certain tasks as "naturally" the work of men, while other tasks are essentially "women's work." More is at stake than simple *difference*, though. For, when such distinctions are deeply inscribed in individual selves, they almost always involve invidious distinctions that congeal in starkly drawn *inequalities* as well. In an effort to make sense of such gender inequalities, feminists have sometimes invoked the concept of "patriarchy," or institutionalized systems that compel women to submit to control by men. From this perspective, then, the question is how these systems work, what forms they take in different societies, and why they weaken in some places but not in others.[3]

Feminist approaches toward work see such arrangements as marked by five critical features. First, they are *arbitrary* social constructs that cannot be reduced to physiology. This is why a given occupation can be defined as "women's work" in one society, but as "men's work" in another. Indeed, Boston College sociologist Leslie Salzinger (2003) has shown how sharply conceptions of gender and women workers' bodies can vary even across factories located within a single region of Mexico. It is also why societies typically invoke powerful sanctions or penalties for people who transgress – apparently, social intervention is often needed just to make sure that "nature" makes good on its promises. Social scientists typically use the term "gender" to capture the culturally fashioned distinctions between men and women – distinctions that are often so deeply inscribed in our institutions and our bodies that we take them to be expressions of our biological make-up.

Second, and as suggested above, these distinctions are not only separate but also starkly *unequal*. This is why jobs that come to be viewed as "women's work" are almost always more poorly rewarded than work viewed as "men's work," even when we control for skill requirements and labor-market scarcity (matters discussed in chapter 4 of this volume). Sociologists Maria Charles and David Grusky (2004) refer to this as the "male primacy" assumption – a tenacious doctrine that defines men as more "status-worthy" and competent in the exercise of authority than women. It is also why the desegregation of occupations tends to operate in one direction, with women readily entering into previously all-male occupations but few men wishing to embark on occupational paths that have historically been defined as "women's work." This pattern reflects not only material considerations (women's pay is so much lower), but also cultural influences (men's identity suffers a symbolic assault when they perform women's work).

Third, the gendering of work is *ubiquitous*, or omnipresent. Gender segregation at work remains a prevalent feature of the US occupational structure; and, indeed, the preponderance of men and women in the paid labor force are employed at jobs that are held by members of their own gender. There are indeed few jobs (or for that matter technologies or even cultural objects) that do not in some way have subtle associations inscribed within them that signify their masculine or feminine nature. Despite much litigation, the sexual division of labor remains deeply established within virtually all workplaces. Administrative support remains largely a women's domain within most organizations; skilled manual work is not. Service work, which often involves the labor of caring and the expression of emotion, is typically defined as a female domain; the exercise of significant authority in professional and managerial settings (although certainly changing) often remains a predominantly male domain. Indeed, the expansion of the service economy itself is partly rooted in gender dynamics. As women's employment has expanded in such heavily gendered occupations as teaching, social work, and nursing, the result has fueled demand for "female" jobs that had previously been performed at home, thus giving rise to a dramatic expansion of highly gendered jobs in care-giving occupations such as cleaning, cooking, and caring for young children (Macdonald and Merrill 2009: 113). Few men seem willing to enter into these forms of care work even in contexts of extremely high unemployment.

A fourth feature of the sexual division of labor worth noting here is its *resilience*. This is evident with respect to gender divisions within US manufacturing during and after World War II – even when women workers did pour into wartime production, the division of labor within the factories was often reproduced in subtle ways, as men reasserted deep-seated distinctions between men's and women's work that had no material basis or need (Milkman 1987). And, as Charles and Grusky (2004) point out, although the last three decades of the twentieth century have shown a sharp convergence in men's and women's rates of labor-force participation, levels of educational attainment, and beliefs about women's role as political leaders, only modest changes have occurred in the prevalence of occupational segregation by sex. Doctrines of meritocracy and equal opportunity have therefore challenged some forms of gender segregation, but left other forms untouched. Data suggest that, over time, gender segregation at work showed its sharpest decline in those years when the women's movement made its strongest legal and political gains. As mobilization and legal support have waned, however, so too has the pace of gender desegregation, which has largely plateaued.

A fifth feature of work that feminist theory has stressed concerns the *complexity* of gender inequality, which is almost always interwoven with other axes of inequality. This point emerged with great clarity in ethnographic work conducted by British social scientists (Willis 1977, 1979; Cockburn 1983), which has unearthed some of the ways in which gender ideologies have reinforced the class inequalities which working men typically face. Put simply, because men come to view harsh material conditions as part of the "manly confrontation with the task," and often define the ability to withstand such hardship as a test of one's manliness, they implicitly embrace their gender and not class interests. The same point has also emerged in studies by African-American women, who have noted that much feminist research has tended to foreground the experience and situation of white women, thus missing the ways in gender *differentially* affects women of color (Collins 2000; Browne and Misra 2003). More recently, sociologists have sought to understand the ways in which race, class, and gender all intersect, generating hierarchies and distributing opportunities in ways which deviate from what we might expect by viewing each dimension of inequality in isolation from other lines of demarcation. For example, in her ethnographic study of ethnic, gender, and class relations at a California high school, the New School sociologist Julie Bettie (2003) has shown that when Latinas from working-class backgrounds "do" gender at school – e.g., they adopt precociously feminine patterns of dress, make-up, and styles of interaction – they do so in ways that represent the working-out of deep class and ethnic inequalities as well. The Latinas in this study refuse to accept the degrading images their schools often impose on them as working-class Latinas, and perform a stylized version of femininity that effectively challenges the school's authority. Here, ethnicity, class, and gender all combine in highly complex ways. Mindful of this, Northwestern University sociologist Leslie McCall (2001) has advocated careful empirical analysis of the different "configurations of inequality" that congeal in given economic regions of the United States, teasing out how industry, region, and gender all combine to establish different forms of economic inequality.

As revealed in chapter 4, feminist research has developed a powerful body of scholarship that has repeatedly refuted pernicious myths about the "essential" qualities of men and women workers. It has probed into the workings of gender inequality in pay, power, and prestige. It has shown how gender inequality inflects virtually all features of economic life, often in spite of determined efforts to uproot it. And, by showing how gender interacts with other axes of inequality, this literature has contributed a sophisticated understanding of the many forms that gender inequality assumes within varying classes and racial groups. An appreciation of gender inequality at work is in fact one of the signal contributions of American sociology, and represents a particular strength in the study of work. It holds great importance for public policy in ways that have yet to be tapped.[4]

The institutionalist perspective

In one way or another, Marxist, interactionist, and feminist theories of work all focus their attention on the social relations established within the workplace itself. Although none is at all blind to the play of wider social forces, each sees much of the "action" shaping work as taking place within the firm as such.

A fourth and last perspective breaks with this assumption. It does so by stressing the *external* influences and constraints – especially, legal, political, and cultural aspects of the environment – that impinge on the structure of work organizations. Put differently, theorists in the institutionalist camp emphasize the myriad ways in which organizational environments shape the structure of work, compelling managers and executives to conform to deeply held expectations rooted well beyond the organization's walls. The institutionalist view has gained further prominence in recent years, especially among sociologists employed within business schools. It commands our attention here for at least two reasons. First, it begins to explain why organizational elites often show more concern with wider public perceptions of the firm than with the knowledge and inclinations of their own employees. Although Marxist theorists would view such unresponsiveness as an expression of class-based inequalities, institutionalists offer a different explanation. Second, some institutionalists have proposed a powerful argument about the future of work and the rise of the "flexible" firm that cannot go ignored.

On the face of it, organizations seem sharply distinct from their wider social and cultural environments. Especially in the post-9/11 world, ID badges are needed to enter many workplaces and security guards scrutinize the movements (and sometimes even the persons) of each visitor seeking entry into secure facilities. Laws stipulate that employers cannot ask about the personal or private lives of prospective employees. Yet, in many ways, the boundary between the workplace and the wider social world is highly deceptive. As two major institutional theorists have put it, social and cultural environments "penetrate the organization, creating the lenses through which actors view the world and the very categories of structure, action, and thought employees use to carry out the firm's work" (DiMaggio and Powell 1991: 13).

Why this should be so is that decision-makers are perpetually faced with uncertainty, and thus strongly motivated to find established models of how to approach novel situations. Moreover, managers are keenly aware of the importance of maintaining the legitimacy of their organization in the eyes of powerful external audiences. Especially among larger, highly visible firms, the circulation of negative views about an organization can have massive effects on its prospects of securing vital resources. Firms must often walk something of a tightrope. They must distinguish themselves from their competitors, but they must at the same time conform to what are widely recognized as the trappings of corporate excellence. For this reason, as firms become established within particular sectors or branches of production, as managers interact with one another across company boundaries, and as employees migrate from firm to firm, what results are powerful tendencies that compel organizations to conform by adopting widely shared codes and practices – that is, to become isomorphic with one another. The point of the institutionalist perspective, then, is that organizations are not isolated entities responding to market demands. Rather, they are embedded within distinct organizational fields that often bring powerful normative influences to bear on the business practices that individual firms adopt (DiMaggio and Powell 1983; Meyer and Rowan 1977). In the words of John Meyer and Richard Scott: "Environments are more than stocks of resources and energy flows; they are cultural systems, defining and legitimating organizational structures and thus aiding in their creation and maintenance." Thus organizations are both "connected to" and "constructed by" their wider, societal environments much more firmly than it might appear (Meyer and Scott 1992: 1).

Multiple studies have emerged that attest to the power of the normative order that surrounds and informs organizational life. Harvard sociologist Frank Dobbin (1994) has shown how the cultural ideals found within France, Great Britain, and the United States shaped the system of industrial regulation that unfolded in each society. The spread of "due process" systems of personnel administration, complete with internal job ladders and formal procedures for hiring from within, was not a response to economic or labor-market conditions, but a response on the part of large, highly visible corporations to the rise of the civil rights movement and the anti-discrimination laws the US Congress began to pass from 1964 onwards (Sutton et al. 1994; Edelman 1990). Likewise, the spread of the multidivisional form of corporate structure after World War I was significantly informed by the influence of large firms that diffused across whole industries, quite independently of financial or economic needs (Fligstein 1985). The point of the institutionalist approach is that organizations are embedded in normative orders and structural fields that exert far-reaching influence over the practices that are adopted within particular firms.

The institutionalist perspective begins to explain why employees so often feel that their concerns are neglected by managers, executives, and organizational elites, and why decision-makers so often seem concerned with potential threats to the perception that obtains outside the firm itself. The reason, institutionalists suggest, is because the fate of the organization may hinge not so much on the technical efficiency of its operations as on the degree to which its structure and practices are deemed to be legitimate in the eyes of powerful constituencies outside the firm. This is cold comfort to workers, of course, who often adopt a cynical view of the managerial inclination to conform to established norms (recall Weeks's study of BritArm, discussed above). Yet, from the institutionalist perspective, there may be no alternative. Firms must operate within particular organizational fields, and must comport with the expectations established therein if they are to succeed.

From this institutionalist perspective, however, there may be some reason to anticipate a happier alignment of employee inclinations and the environment of the firm. The point, some institutionalists contend, is that the structural and cultural environments that surround contemporary organizations have begun to shift in novel directions, leading firms away from their long-standing reliance on centralized bureaucratic forms. In an increasingly knowledge-based economy, for example, firms cannot know with certainty which forms of scientific and technical knowledge they are likely to need for product and process innovation. Especially in dynamic and science-based industries, some research suggests that firms now forgo investing in their own scientific laboratories; rather, they enter into strategic partnerships and product-specific alliances, or utilize network ties that provide the knowledge and information they need (Powell et al. 1996; Saxenian 1994). Indeed, the Stanford economic sociologist Walter Powell (1990) has suggested that the network form has emerged as a functional alternative to either markets or centralized hierarchies, with many virtues that the latter structures cannot provide. Moreover, as the employment opportunities of knowledge workers begin to expand, employees cease forming lifelong attachments to a given *firm*, instead forming allegiances to their *occupation*. The result generates a growing pool of expert workers who are able to become practitioners on their own terms, with fewer of the constraints traditionally imposed by administrative rigidities. To describe this development, the management theorists Michael Arthur and Denise Rousseau (2001) have coined the term "boundaryless career," by which they mean occupational trajectories that no longer constrain workers within a single firm, but instead anchor them within more flexible arrangements rooted either in their occupation, a spatial locale, or both.

This species of institutionalist theory is in some respects unique. Like other forms of institutionalist theory, those of the knowledge economy emphasize the ways in which the structures of work organizations are shaped by the social and economic environment. Unlike other variants on the institutionalist theme, however, they operate with a clear conception of organizational change and the path down which firms are likely to head. This may be both the strength and the weakness of this particular approach. It emphasizes the structural demands of the knowledge economy, and tries to foresee the myriad changes in organizational structure and career trajectories that are likely to unfold in the contemporary era (matters discussed in more detail in chapter 3). These are vital tasks for any sociology of work – and not ones that have been sufficiently addressed. Yet, in trying to theorize the nature of the new period in which work is likely to unfold, theorists of the knowledge economy have been quick to assume that older issues that have plagued work organizations – most notably, the problem of inequality and domination – tend to recede into the past. Arguably, this last perspective contains elements of a futuristic and even utopian quality that limit the validity of its predictions.

Conclusion

It is important to avoid exaggerating the differences among the four perspectives outlined above. For one thing, there are important sources of divergence internal to each of these theoretical camps. For another, many scholars have sought to borrow themes from each approach, generating perspectives that actively defy the categories sketched out above. Marxist theorists have at times sought to borrow from the interactionist emphasis on the self, for example, and have at times drawn attention to the fusion of class and gender influences. For their part, feminists have increasingly utilized the notion of gender as a performance (a theme initially developed within the work of Erving Goffman). And institutionalists have at times drawn on interactionist themes (Bearman 2005). Other instances of cross-fertilization can likewise be found, generating insights that have greatly enriched and expanded our understanding of work.

Though it is fashionable to mock academic debates and tempting to dismiss theoretical thinking as idle speculation, such an approach can be self-defeating. For how we think about work, how we see the forces that define our work situations, what issues we define as needing public attention, and what claims we can legitimately make of our jobs – all these and other issues are quite real and have important consequences for us all. The point is that theory is an essential element in thinking about work (among other phenomena), for it leads us to define certain things as problematic and thus as in need of explanation. There are often practical and political consequences that flow from the way we think about work, in other words, and this should be kept firmly in mind.

Moreover, it is important to note that the sociology of work does not develop in a vacuum. Rather, how we conceive of work is inevitably affected by the flux of economic and political events. Marxist theories of the labor process (discussed below in chapter 2) found their greatest influence in an era following the surge of labor unrest and economic uncertainty that began in the late 1960s and continued until the early 1980s. With the rise of new forms of economic competition and organization (the Japanese challenge, the rise of Silicon Valley, and then the dot.com boom in the 1990s), a general turn toward business-oriented conceptions of economic activity seemed to gain currency, and institutionalist arguments rose to greater prominence (as is discussed in chapter 3). In some respects, we have yet to break free of such perspectives, which seem if anything to have gained greater strength as a result of the financial crisis and economic contraction that began in 2007. The social environment and political culture shape the concepts that researchers find plausible, in ways that we do well to inspect.

Yet the environment does not shape us in a unilateral way. People – workers, union leaders, and social movement activists – can at times have a major impact on the structure of work and the public policies that govern workplace life. Much of the stability and security that work eventually came to provide was in fact the product of the workers' movement, which won major concessions from corporate employers by the end of World War II, gaining legal and organizational protections that expanded workers' rights in far-reaching ways (the bumper sticker says it all: "The Weekend: Brought to You by the Labor Movement"). Personnel and human resources practices that provide a measure of protection against arbitrary and capricious decisions at work also represent corporate responses to the women's and civil rights movements, which have begun to address the ascriptive inequalities that unfold along gender and racial lines (as discussed in chapters 4 and 5). More recent efforts to shape the structure and context of work have often focused on the globalization of work. Here can be found an ongoing struggle between advocates of neo-liberal approaches toward the global economy (led by economic policymakers and corporate elites), and efforts to direct globalization down alternative paths (as advocated by transnational activist networks, anti-sweatshop movements, and human rights organizations). The outcome of this latter struggle (the focus of chapter 6) is likely to shape the nature of work for decades to come, both in the developed and developing world alike. Whether new sources of mobilization are likely to arise – among the long-term unemployed? Fueled by social media? Driven by students saddled with insurmountable debts and few employment prospects? – remains to be seen.

2

Capitalism, Taylorism, and the Problem of Labor Control

One of the more provocative strands of social-scientific thinking about work during the last quarter of the twentieth century was that of the labor-process school. Linking Marxist concepts to historical and ethnographic research, labor-process analysts opened up lines of inquiry that previous generations of thinkers had failed to pursue. For example, rather than taking for granted the existence of managerial prerogatives (as if highly centralized authority were part of the natural order of things), adherents of the labor-process school asked a series of probing questions about why authority and control over work is so unilaterally bestowed upon managers. Where previous generations of thinkers had viewed workplace technology as an autonomous, self-generating force that stood above or beyond social and political influences, labor-process thinkers insisted on interrogating the social processes that underlie the design, selection, and use of particular machine designs (Noble 1984; Thomas 1994). In place of the benign image of centralized managerial hierarchies that mainstream social science had embraced, adherents of the labor-process school raised far-reaching questions about the distribution of power and authority within work organizations, and about the ways in which work reflected class inequality writ large. In all these respects it filled a sociological void.

Yet, in recent years, labor process theory has quite clearly been thrown on the defensive, as its core arguments and concerns have grown "unfashionable," as Berkeley sociologist Michael Burawoy laments (1985). In this chapter, I develop a reconsideration of the labor-process school, warts and all, the better to take stock of its virtues and limitations. As such, I address one of the school's central concerns – the problem of managerial control over work and workers. Put simply: how has it been possible for employers to maintain their control over labor in spite of the deeply conflicting interests that capital and labor bring to bear on the labor process? I contend that adherents of the labor-process school have essentially given three overlapping answers to this question. The first, led by Braverman, focused on Taylorism (or scientific management), and gave rise to a debate over the "de-skilling" of work. A second answer veered in a more cultural direction, and emphasized the symbolic or normative controls that workers typically encounter at work. A third and most recent answer has emphasized the ways in which work organizations have in effect begun to colonize workers' identities, with companies making claims on aspects of the worker's being that had previously stood beyond corporate control.

Reviewing the unfolding of these debates reveals much that is of enduring value. The labor-process school has contributed a great deal to our understanding of work – and certainly more, theoretically and empirically, than its mainstream critics have allowed. It has also steadfastly sought to challenge the myth of classlessness that anesthetizes so much of everyday life. Still, it seems clear that a significant reorientation is needed if this approach is to capture the major features of workplace change on the horizon today. Such discussion is all the more urgent in view of the multiple forms of restructuring that are currently under way in the contemporary capitalist economy.

Taylorism and the De-skilling Debate

Marx himself wrote a fair amount on the nature of the labor process (1967 [1865]). His analyses of the movement from artisanal labor to Modern Industry, the struggle over the length of the working day, the relation between machinery and workers, and the division between mental and manual labor all remain important contributions. Yet, surprisingly perhaps, the generations of Marxist thinkers who followed after Marx showed little abiding interest in these themes, or in the actual contours of work. Some, such as Karl Kautsky, Rosa Luxemburg, Rudolf Hilferding, and Paul Sweezy, were far more concerned with the system of capital accumulation rather than with the conditions of employment workers encountered in any given industry or region. Others, such as Georg Lukács and Louis Althusser, addressed abstract philosophical questions such as the relative merits of Hegelian thought and the proper method of interpretating Marx's texts. A notable void existed with respect to the application of Marxist thinking, and the labor-process school rushed to fill this gap.

And, for a time, the context augured well. There was reason to believe that the period of labor quiescence that emerged in the decades after World War II was coming to an abrupt halt (as evident in the explosive wave of strikes that gripped both France and Italy at the end of the 1960s, and that found echoes in the United States). For another, a new generation of scholars had emerged that was beginning to challenge the benign image of industrial society that had predominated within the academy. In Britain, scholars such as E. P. Thompson and Eric Hobsbawm opened up new lines of scholarly inquiry with respect to working-class history. Their counterparts in the United States (especially David Montgomery and David Brody) challenged the doctrine of American exceptionalism, which had propounded a highly misleading, quiescent conception of US labor history.

This was the setting in which the labor-process school first emerged. It drew particular inspiration from Harry Braverman's *Labor and Monopoly Capital* (1974), a massive work that trained a Marxist lens on the history of work. A metalworker turned labor journalist and journal editor, Braverman operated on the assumption that, under capitalism, employers faced two enduring obstacles to the expansion of their businesses. One was the cost of production and the problem of minimizing wages. The other was the problem of controlling unruly workers (more strictly speaking, of maximizing their use of the labor power employers had purchased). The problem of cost demanded that employers perpetually seek out ways of subdividing labor – of reorganizing skilled tasks into their constituent elements. Braverman called this imperative the "Babbage principle," after the British economist who wrote extensively on the topic two centuries ago. The problem of control, in Braverman's analysis, was made all the more vexing when employers faced highly skilled or knowledgeable employees. For under these conditions, the company continued to depend on the workers' own methods and technical expertise. Such conditions set intolerable limits on the prospect for capitalist expansion, and compelled employers to find some recourse.

How could such obstacles be overcome? The answer Braverman gave is implied in his very formulation of the problem. Since employers could never seize full control of production so long as workers remained in possession of strategic production knowledge, the answer must lie in the effort to transform the distribution of skill and production knowledge within the firm itself. This was precisely the task that fell to the scientific management (or Taylorist) movement at the end of the nineteenth century.[1] Although historians continue to debate Taylorism's actual legacy (Stark 1980; Guillen 1994; Montgomery 1987), there is nothing equivocal about Braverman's interpretation: he finds in Taylorism the purest expression ever devised of the laws governing the capitalist division of labor. What Taylor advised employers to do was to uproot the time-encrusted thicket of customary, craft-dependent practices that governed the work process. By ruthlessly using the methods of the natural sciences to study workers' jobs, employers could develop their own body of production knowledge, and use this knowledge to devise the "one best way" for conducting each task. Such an approach presupposed the sharp separation between the work of "conception" and "execution." Planning, analyzing, and designing would all be concentrated in the hands of management; mere execution (the carrying out of directives from above) would henceforward be the domain of the workers. In this view, the significance of Taylorism lay in its explicit declaration of the core organizing principle that was to shape the structure of work; it was "the most decisive single step in the division of labor taken by the capitalist model of production" (1974: 126). Initially deployed within the nation's manufacturing plants, this principle soon found application to office and clerical work, and then to the burgeoning service occupations. Driven not only by the need to minimize labor costs, but also by the need to limit the workers' capacity to resist their own subordination, employers gave rise to a relentless tendency toward the "degradation" or de-skilling of labor, which cheapened work and emptied it of all meaning and autonomy.

There is no need to reiterate the lines of critical discussion that Braverman's theory provoked, other than to make the following points. The most obvious and frequently lamented shortcoming of his formulation is its overarching *determinism*. His is a model in which capital has the power to act; for its part, labor has no recourse but to obey (Stark 1980; Littler and Salaman 1982). Thus began an ongoing discussion over the relation between structure and agency and the efficacy of worker resistance that continues to this day. Related is a further point: the highly pronounced *moralism* that informs his analysis, leading it to selectively invoke evidence in favor of the de-skilling thesis while ignoring countervailing trends. This is perhaps why some critics have accused de-skilling theorists of romanticizing older forms of labor, and of viewing Taylor as the "serpent in the craftsman's paradise" (Monds 1976). Perhaps the most serious limitation afflicting Braverman's analysis is his *materialism* – that is, his undue reliance on economic relations, at the expense of any attention to social, cultural, or institutional influences on the structure of work. This combination of shortcomings led Braverman to fasten on a single characteristic of work – possession of production knowledge, or skill – as the critical factor mediating the distribution of control within the labor process.

This last point – his tendency to inflate the importance of skill – was especially unfortunate, since it directed much of the labor process down what in retrospect constitutes a dead end. The question of trends in skill requirements surely holds significance for educational policy, for job-training programs, and for labor and employee relations research as well. *Yet the crux of labor-process theory hinges on the question of control, not of skill.* Although workers who wield scarce production knowledge and expertise can at times wield power as a result – especially where labor market conditions allow this – cases abound in which the possession of skill has little or no purchase on control at work, whether because such skills are unrecognized or invisible, or else because workers lack the social and organizational capacity to make their preferences felt.

Despite its manifest flaws – and in spite of its "unfashionable" status – it seems important to point out some of the ways in which early labor-process analysis anticipated important developments. Taylorism itself has remained influential in the design of production processes, most especially in the form of "lean production" – Toyota's appropriation of the Taylorist legacy, which (despite its emphasis on teamwork) takes the quantification and intensification of work to levels that Taylor never imagined (see Dohse, Jürgens, and Malsch 1985; Berggren 1992). Indeed, lean production has now given rise to "lean retailing" and to the Walmart-led "logistics revolution," all of which have accelerated the movement of commodities through the value chain and placed control of the production process ever further from the worker's grasp. Ironically, in its August 4, 2009, edition, the *Wall Street Journal* reported that one of the bastions of "latte capitalism" – Starbucks itself – has instituted a vice president of "lean thinking":

> Pushing Starbuck's drive is Scott Heydon, the company's "vice president of lean thinking," and a student of the Toyota production system, where lean manufacturing got its start. He and a 10-person "lean team" have been going from region to region armed with a stopwatch and a Mr. Potato Head toy that they challenge managers to put together and re-box in less than 45 seconds.

Yet everything depends on the significance we attach to these corporate initiatives. For one thing, the literature on lean production itself suggests that although it advances a more sophisticated engineering conception of work, it remains vulnerable to the same strategies and tactics of resistance that workers have historically invoked (see Graham 1995; Vallas 2006). For another, in the case of Starbucks, we must still acknowledge the importance of interactive service work and the store/worker/customer triangle as a feature that even the most ingenious Mr Potato Head exercise cannot address. The

point is that between the structural attributes of the labor
process and the outcomes management seeks inevitably lies
a thick layer of perception, governed by normative influences
and collective identities that no Taylorist manual alone can
design. This point recalls the principle established in chapter
1, alluding to the hidden underside of work, and the ways in
which workers can informally resist, subvert, or challenge
managerial edicts – matters that have by now attracted a
sizeable body of literature (Hodson 1995; Simpson 1989;
Knights and McCabe 2000; Vallas 2003c).

Seeking to transcend models of the labor process that are
(as in Braverman's case) all structure and no agency, analysts have moved to explore the social, cultural, and political
means through which employers have sought to gain control
over the labor process, quite independently of the distribution
of skill and production expertise.

Workplace Culture and Managerial Control

This movement has been a halting and uneven effort. One
of the more fertile efforts to advance labor-process theory
beyond the de-skilling cul-de-sac was advanced by Richard
Edwards, an economist who articulated an influential historical typology of corporate control over work (1979). Several
of the types that Edwards identified did rest on material structures. By "simple" control, Edwards referred to the arbitrary
power that supervisors could (and can) wield in the absence
of formal constraints. By "technical" control, he had in mind
the shifting of control into the material underpinnings of the
production process (such as with assembly-line production),
which comes to enforce a given method and pace of work.
But Edwards's third type – bureaucratic control – began to
acknowledge the role of culture and ideology, in that normative elements play a larger role in this third system of
employer control than do the others in Edwards's schema.
Thus, under bureaucratic control, workers find themselves
embedded within complex webs of rules and expectations
that act as powerful constraints on workers' actions and allegiances. Job descriptions define workers' tasks in elaborate
detail. Employee handbooks establish formal systems for

worker evaluations; and systems emerge outlining the sanctions to be invoked when the firm's expectations are not met. Undergirded by the proliferation of job ladders (internal labor markets that reward commitment to the firm), workers begin to identify with the firm, rather than with fellow employees.

This nascent recognition of the power of normative constructs was more fully developed in subsequent work by the Berkeley sociologist Michael Burawoy, whose *Manufacturing Consent* (1979) provided a robust theoretical basis for labor-process research. Burawoy serendipitously wound up conducting participant observation research in the same machine-tool shop in which Donald Roy had worked a quarter-century before (see chapter 1). Some of the same aspects of workshop culture persisted, but with a few significant changes. For one thing, this establishment had been acquired by a large Fortune 500 conglomerate, and had thus already incorporated some of the features of bureaucratic control that Edwards stressed. But what was most decisive, Burawoy found, was the nature of the shop-floor culture that workers established in an effort to cope with their unrewarding work situations. Partly in response to the piece-rate payment system used by the company, workers construed their work as a game – "making out" – whose participants in effect competed to demonstrate their skill and prowess in mastering even the most difficult of production assignments. At times, the game made work tolerable, in that it provided a source of meaning in an otherwise harsh and unforgiving environment. But the consequence of playing this game was that it induced participants to adapt to the difficult and even abusive conditions in which they were employed. That is, the culture of making out established an ideological ensemble or subculture that invited workers to consent to their own exploitation.

In subsequent writings, Burawoy sought to develop the theoretical implications of his initial findings, using the resulting schema to inform comparative-historical analysis of the labor process in a more ambitious way (1985). Although his thinking is complex, the most salient contribution this work made lay in its effort to focus more clearly on the social conditions that underpin the exercise of power-over labor. He did this in three distinct ways. First, he introduced a set of concepts aimed at capturing the most salient features of workplace life. Dissatisfied with using such Marxist abstractions as the relations *of* production, he insists on speaking of the relations *in* production – a term by which he means the forms of interaction that surround and define the exercise of power at work, and that often shape and constrain working-class responses to the employer. Second, he introduces a complex typology of the "factory regimes" that have emerged since the rise of competitive capitalism. As part of his argument here, he chides Marx for fastening on a single type of factory regime – that which Burawoy dubs "market despotism" – to the exclusion of other, less obviously coercive types. Related here is a third point: that the wider social and political conditions in which contemporary regimes exist has altered their character. Because the labor process is somewhat more fully regulated than before, and social insurance systems provide at least a modicum of subsistence independently of the wage, workers are no longer so completely dependent on the sale of their labor power for subsistence. Under these conditions, Burawoy foresees a broad historical shift from "despotic" to "hegemonic" types of production regimes – that is, from reliance on sheer *coercion*, to relations in production that emphasize *consent* (though never entirely to the exclusion of coercion). In effect, Burawoy concludes that the cultural ensemble he unearthed in his Chicago machine shop was indicative of a broader phenomenon, in which hegemonic production regimes underpin managerial control.

Burawoy's thinking was influential, and part of a broader, ongoing turn toward ethnographic studies that sought to take seriously the role that workplace culture plays in the production of employee consent. Expressions of this movement have steadily grown. The work of MIT ethnographer John van Maanen and his colleagues has been especially important. Van Maanen's (1991) classic analysis of work in Disneyland ("The Smile Factory") stands as one example. Workers at Disneyland are not paid well. Their work day is arduous and long. They must wear what from any reasoned perspective are silly costumes. And they are often rudely treated by customers ("guests") and supervisors. And yet, so powerful is the Disney culture that employees routinely submit to the demands of their jobs and firmly stay in character long past the call of duty. Indeed, so compelling is the status structure

at Disneyland that the characters employees play have powerful effects on their dating patterns, often overwhelming the
class positions they hold beyond Disneyland's gates. As Van
Maanen puts it, "identities are not so much dismantled as
they are set aside as employees are schooled in the use of new
identities of the situational sort" (1991: 21). These new identities are often so demanding, moreover, that to manage them
requires employees to put their actions on "automatic pilot,"
or to "go robot," as a means of coping with the stresses of
their performances (cf. Leidner 1993). The analysis here is
not so much of despotism as of dramaturgy, but it demonstrates the power of normative control over workplace life.

This argument is advanced in a different form, and with a
different focus, by Van Maanen's student, the Israeli anthropologist Gideon Kunda (1992). Conducting a masterful study
of "High Tech," a prominent Silicon Valley firm, he seeks to
demonstrate the ways in which workplace culture can engage
and absorb the energies and affiliations of workers in the
knowledge economy. The executives at High Tech are themselves keenly aware of the importance of the culture concept,
and consciously set out to develop a rich and robust way of
life that can encompass and inspire all employees. The firm
even hires culture specialists, whose job is that of the production, maintenance, and repair of the normatively controlled
world in which employees work. Employees are themselves
conscious of management's designs, but so firmly immersed
in the need to use the meaning-system the firm has elaborated
as to be capable of little more than scattered cynicism as an
expression of dissent. Those who fail at work are not let go
– High Tech has a no-layoff policy – but retained, cast in the
role of the tragic hero, and used as walking examples of the
need to take risks.

Other uses of the culture concept have fastened on the
introduction of new, seemingly egalitarian, forms of work
organization. This is a large and still-growing literature.
An early expression of this tradition was the 1988 study by
Guillermo Grenier, the New Mexico sociologist who studied
a medical instruments plant in Arizona. This plant introduced
a team-based work system, which it framed as an instance
of its concern for employee fulfillment. In fact, the system
operated as a means of subordinating workers, forestalling

self-organization on the workers' part, and delegating to them the work of supervising other employees. This critical strand of research on team systems has accumulated in a large number of case studies, including James Barker's (1993) study of an electronics plant and Laurie Graham's (1995) study of a Japanese-managed truck assembly plant in Indiana, to name but a few. The notion underlying these studies runs largely parallel to Burawoy's argument. Where labor-control systems under earlier periods of capitalism focused largely on the effort to direct workers' *behavior*, the nascent post-Fordist regimes aim to shape workplace *culture*, now in accordance with management's needs.

Questions could and should be raised about the conceptual formulations that have informed this normative turn. To begin with, dissonant notions of control have emerged in this literature. Thus, the Van Maanen-Kunda strand of research operates with a Durkheimian or Goffmanian lens, in which culture is viewed as a system of ritualized performances. By contrast, Burawoy and others rely on a Gramscian conception of culture as managerial hegemony. Still, despite this variation, it seems clear that the normative approach marks two important advances beyond the de-skilling approach. First, it has shed the earlier reliance on an unduly materialist approach, and thus can trace the subtle yet significant connections between managerial control and the culture established at work. And, second, it has shed the moralism that afflicted the de-skilling school and that led it to romanticize older images of labor. A more sociologically adequate account of managerial control thus begins to come into view.

Workers as Subjects: Governing the Worker's Soul

In recent years, labor-process analysts have extended research on the politics of workplace culture by paying particular attention to the relation between the demands of the work situation and worker subjectivity – that is, the worker's identity. Key to the complex strands of literature that have emerged on this front is the realization that the exercise of control over the labor process cannot be concerned with the normative environment that surrounds the worker; instead, the thrust for control must often reach into or shape the personal attributes of the worker as well. The struggle for control is thus extended into the worker's soul.

One of the most influential works in this connection was that by the Berkeley sociologist Arlie Hochschild, whose *The Managed Heart* (1983) opened up a burgeoning literature on the distinctive demands that service work often places on the workers who perform it. Part of the novelty of Hochschild's argument stemmed from her realization that human emotions are not self-generated, but are in fact the product of norms and expectations – "feeling rules" – that define appropriate reactions in any given situation. Being a competent member of a given society requires that we develop the ability to manage our emotions in accordance with normative demands. In many service occupations, however, firms seek to utilize this human capacity for emotion-management, now transforming it into an instrument of commerce. In such settings, workers must perform what Hochschild calls "emotional labor" – that is, they must engage in bodily and verbal displays of emotion as a condition of their employment. Work acquires a performative aspect, in which the presentation of self and the expression of commercially appropriate feelings become central features of the worker's job. Hochschild uses the case of airline flight attendants as her major case in point. On the basis of interviews and observations, she reveals just how elaborate an effort the employer must make in order to ensure that flight attendants smile sincerely and convey convincing levels of concern and care in relation to their passengers.

Drawing partly on Marx's theory of alienation, and partly on Goffman's analysis of interpersonal rituals, Hochschild draws attention to the human dilemmas that the performance of emotional labor creates. Because service workers must publicly manufacture feelings that are not genuinely their own, a subtle yet gnawing form of self-estrangement begins to arise. Put simply, employees quite rightly come to see that their emotional equipment is no longer entirely their own (Leidner 1993). In Hochschild's words, "when the product – the thing to be engineered, mass produced, and subjected to speed-up and slowdown – is a smile, a mood, a feeling, or a relationship, it comes to belong more to the organization and less to the self" (1983: 198). Implied here is an important point: a new terrain – the worker's self – has in effect become subject to commercial development and appropriation (Grugulis, Dundon, and Wilkinson 2000).

Hochschild's study has served to stimulate a wealth of studies focused on the distinctive features of interactive service occupations. In this respect, she served to expand labor-process analysis well beyond its traditional emphasis upon manual or manufacturing work. Indeed, much of the resulting literature has engaged in ongoing debate about the nature of service work as distinct from industrial work. One source of distinction lies in the object of the service worker's labor, which by its very nature is work that is performed on human beings, who must ordinarily be present during the transaction itself (though technology introduces complexities in the nature of this presence). A further point is that service work cannot easily be stored or outsourced (a point that has implications for the distribution of power within given industries). Further, since service work usually entails a face-to-face performance, it often acquires elements of unpredictability in spite of the most robust effort at scripting and structuring the service encounter. A final point, emphasized by Hochschild herself, is that the worker's appearance and expressed identity or disposition themselves become part and parcel of the "product" as such. The cash-nexus thus claims regions of the social world that had previously been distant from direct economic exchange (Korczynski and Macdonald 2009).

An additional point that has been emphasized in the literature on service work is that the presence of the customer within the labor process renders the pursuit of managerial control much more complex than in manufacturing labor processes. In structural terms, the geometry of control has changed (Leidner 1993; Orr 1996; Korczynski 2009). In place of the *dyadic* form that characterized industrial production (where the chief axis of inequality is that between manager and worker), a *triadic* or triangular form dominates the structure of service work, which now requires the coordinated actions of three parties – the employer, the worker, and the customer (or, depending on the institutional context, the patient, client, guest, student, inmate, etc.). The key question here concerns the various forms that this triangular relationship assumes, and how workers cope with the configurations of control they confront during the course of their work.

One answer has been given by the University of Pennsylvania sociologist Robin Leidner (1993). Leidner compared the configuration that the service encounter assumes within two starkly different occupational contexts: that of fast-food workers and door-to-door insurance salesmen. She found that in the former case (that of McDonald's), the employer in effect effaces the worker's identity, replacing it with a standardized and scripted self-presentation that in effect aligns the role of the customer with that of management. Here, the customer and the employer "co-manage" the worker's actions. This compels the service worker to play a polite and pleasant yet avowedly deferential role. In the case of the insurance salesmen, however, the service encounter takes a distinctly different form. Since door-to-door sales work happens off-site, employers must more actively shape the employee's world-view, and are often compelled to develop a host of charismatic controls that engulf or redefine the employee's self (one worker kept a Post-it note on his dashboard that reminded him to "Be Kevin"). Such engulfment enables the company to create an alliance with its sales force, now forming common cause in relation to the customer. In both these cases, however, workers must in effect "wear" a company-provided self, with effects that often confound or corrode conceptions of authentic interaction that are held by the worker and the customer alike.

A recent turn in the literature has begun to fasten on the effects of the marketplace on the service worker's self, but viewed from a somewhat different vantage point. One of the most energetic and creative advocates of this view is the British scholar Paul du Gay (1996; see also du Gay and Salaman 1992; Rose 1990), who perceives a structural trend at work, driven by shifts in the broader culture and polity, that begins to make even greater claims on the identities of workers in retail or service settings than Hochschild and Leidner had allowed.

Basing his argument on a study of retail stores in the UK, Du Gay makes three interrelated claims. First, the demands of the "sovereign consumer" have gained increasing purchase on the structure of business organizations. As demand for mass-produced goods has declined, firms must continually strive to accommodate the ongoing flux in consumer tastes. This disrupts or destabilizes centralized bureaucracies, prompting the development of more "flexible" forms of organizational control (see chapter 3). Second, as neo-liberal policies have triumphed over traditions favoring the welfare state, the logic of the marketplace has increasingly flowed into work organizations, infusing the "discourse of enterprise" into the innermost recesses of the firm. Du Gay points out that many of the newer forms of work organization (such as Total Quality Management and Just-in-Time delivery systems) actively encourage firms to define their internal operations in terms of the customer/supplier relationship. Third, these developments induce employers to redefine the personal attributes they expect of their employees, producing a correlative shift in the forms of subjectivity that contemporary firms seek to inscribe within their employees.

For du Gay, the exercise of power operates in large part by institutionalizing discourses that gain purchase on the worker's self. As he puts it, "forms of power 'work' by constructing and maintaining the forms of subjectivity most appropriate to a given type of social practice" (1996: 54). Thus firms are increasingly compelled to elicit from their employees the personal attributes that the new conditions demand.

> Rather than being some vague, incalculable 'spirit', the culture of enterprise is inscribed within a variety of mechanisms – application forms, recruitment 'auditions', communication groups and the like – through which senior management . . . seek to delineate, normalize, and instrumentalize the conduct of persons in order to achieve the ends they postulate as desirable. (du Gay 1996: 61)

The result is the generation of subtle yet powerful norms that define the cognitive, affective, and personal attributes by which employees are evaluated. Employers therefore cultivate employees who willingly conform to marketplace norms – that is, "enterprising subjects" – aligning their selfhood with the organization's needs (see also Casey 1995; Vallas and Hill, forthcoming).

The infusion of market discourse into the firm reshapes not only workers' world-views, but also their personal style. Especially in the hospitality industries, a key part of the worker's job performance rests in his or her ability to communicate an aesthetic, cultural, or class-based sensibility that embodies the image or "brand" the firm wishes to project. This means that a previously peripheral feature of the employee's self-presentation – the ability to project aesthetic tastes and personal style – becomes subject to the firm's demands. This is the point made by the British organizational theorist Chris Warhurst and his colleagues (Warhurst and Nickson 2007; Nickson and Warhurst 2007; Witz, Warhurst, and Nickson 2003), who speak of the rise of "aesthetic labor," now alongside the performance of emotional labor. Studying upscale hotels, restaurants, entertainment clubs, and retail stores, they find that managers are often more focused on the worker's self-presentation, pattern of speech, fashion, make-up, and physical appearance than on the technical skills and experience they bring with them to the job. In effect, workers become sign vehicles, whose style and appearance come quite literally to embody the corporate brand.

The interview and survey data that Warhurst and his colleagues report suggests that employers in the hospitality industries often focus detailed attention on the worker's hairstyle, make-up, speech code, physical attractiveness, and fashion sense, and even maintain formal policies (including training and evaluation systems) on precisely these points. They also conclude that managing aesthetic labor is not merely a matter of employee selection. Rather, firms actively seek to *produce* the desired employee traits. Thus, at one upscale hotel, workers were given a 10-day induction process that refashioned their hairstyles, make-up, and command of cultural tastes. Moreover, in many of the upscale stores and hotels these scholars studied, aesthetic workers gained a certain measure of freedom or power in relation to the customer (Warhurst and Nickson 2007). Workers in designer retail stores, for example, have sometimes worked as fashion models, and in any event serve as avatars of cultural styles and tastes – a fact that often gives them an elevated status in relation to their customers (see Sherman 2007).

The literature discussed in this section, though disparate

in some respects, shares the assertion that interactive service work represents something new. As the social theorist Daniel Bell put it (1973: xx), where older labor processes approximated either a "game against nature" or a "game against fabricated nature," interactive service work is different; it constitutes a "game between persons." Viewed as such, what recent theories equip us to do is to ask how the game is played, what its rules are, and how these rules actively shape the players themselves. To be sure, this literature is in some respects merely suggestive, for we lack the ability to chart the terrain of the many and highly varied branches of the service economy. Still, recent theories begin to suggest a number of points that are valuable.

First, the expansion of the market for upscale consumer services has introduced a widening gulf between the two types of service work that Leidner captured in her study – on the one hand, the low-paying, low-skill jobs that Macdonald and Sirianni (1996: 3) called the "emotional proletariat"; and, on the other hand, the more "empowered" or autonomous worker who plays a larger directive role in the service transaction. If the research of du Gay and Warhurst is any guide, then the expansion of upscale enterprises in the retail and hospitality industries may compel scholars to explore the consequences of what Gabriel (2009) has termed "latte capitalism."

A second point that emerges from this literature concerns the infusion of market-based discourse into the realm of the formal, bureaucratic work organization. As du Gay in particular notes, this implies a weakening of the boundary between production and consumption, and an interweaving of their previously distinct logics. The consequences tend to disrupt the once-stable structures and rules that govern the performance of work. Elements of instability and precarity begin to characterize work to a much greater extent than before. Conceivably, these trends can serve to deepen the firm's grip on worker subjectivity (Willmott 1993). Yet at least some research suggests that the very need for creativity which the new forms of work often require generates selves which are not so easily controlled, and technical and cognitive skills with which workers can at times resist corporate forms of control. We discuss these matters further in chapter 3.

Conclusion

Breaking with generations of thinking that had taken the nature of our economic institutions for granted, the labor-process school posed questions on a crucial area that has been central to the sociology of work. What social arrangements make it possible for employers to control the labor on which their firms rely? How is labor regulated? And what spaces of resistance might be identified in the existing regimes? Scholarly answers have followed a broad arc that has moved from an emphasis on the material conditions of production (the possession of skill and control over workplace technology) to views focused on workplace culture as a vehicle of organizational control, and, finally, to approaches that see organizations as governing through control over workers' subjectivity.

Increasingly, scholars have explored the ways in which management's control and regulation of labor has assumed a normative guise, in which workplace culture begins to police the boundaries of worker behavior. It has fastened on the dilemmas that arise when workers' presentation of self (including their physical appearance) becomes the "product" that is bought and sold. And it has examined the ways in which the norms of consumption and the language of the marketplace have crept into the sphere of production, generating new conceptions of the acceptable self with which workers must conform. These are all highly fruitful lines of analysis that provoke probing questions about the claims that organizations make on employees, especially in an era when market competition seems to require that they increasingly seek to govern our very souls (Rose 1990).

Certainly, it might be objected that normative or cultural controls are hardly sufficient in themselves, and that the very wage-labor relation itself implies an element of economic inequality and coercion that is never far from hand. But certainly, *management* is convinced of the relevance of normative influences, as is evident in the relentless corporate interest in organizational culture, a growing industry in its own right. Indeed, it seems reasonable to conclude that contemporary structural developments have tended to weaken the role of rigid bureaucratic structures, in turn only increasing the importance of normative controls. This is a point that has emerged in some recent studies of workplace change, as in my own studies of both manufacturing and high-tech settings (Vallas 2006).

Above and beyond these observations regarding normative elements of the labor process, several structural developments warrant particular attention here. Three seem especially important: the abandonment of vertically integrated structures (literally, the "disintegration" of the firm), the casualization of the employment relationship, and the financialization of work.

The first tendency – the breaking up or "dis-integration" of the large, vertically integrated structures – would seem to be an endemic feature of global capitalism at this stage in its development (Lash and Urry 1987). As a broad structural trend, it stands to affect a substantial proportion of the labor force, not only domestically but internationally as well. This disintegration can take many forms – the out-sourcing of work to vendors or suppliers external to the firm; redefinitions of the firm's boundaries, excising operations deemed to rest outside the firm's "core" functions; or even what the German sociologist Ulrich Beck (2000) calls the "Brazilianization" of work, which induces workers to move back and forth between formal and informal or insecure employment. It can also stem from many sources. But at the root of much restructuring is the increasingly prevalent belief that vertically integrated hierarchies are no longer economically viable, and that as firms embrace new *strategies* for growth, they must also adopt new *structures* that abandon highly centralized forms of organizational control.

Much of this ferment has centered on the corporate search for "flexibility," a matter to be discussed more fully in the next chapter. What is important to note here are the disruptions that result in the work situations of many employees, as the bureaucratic structures that insulated them against the volatility of the labor market rapidly begin to dissolve. In some cases, the result tends toward polarized outcomes for the workers involved, as workers are sorted into segments who meet different fates. In other cases, workers experience a generalized loss of bureaucratic protections and provisions for career mobility.

Related to this structural disintegration of the firm is a second development, that of the casualization of labor within growing regions of the economy. The concept of "casualization" is especially apt, since it reminds us of the forms of employment (such as the use of day labor and "shape up" rituals) that were highly prevalent in the years before the Great Depression. After the World War II years, most workers in the advanced capitalist societies succeeded in establishing the "standard" work arrangement – access to permanent, full-time employment, with some provision of social benefits – as the "normal" structure that jobs were to assume. Yet, in recent years, large numbers of employers have reversed this course, moving to retreat from the standard work arrangement.

This trend is perhaps best captured in an important discussion by Jeffrey Pfeffer and James Baron (1988), who outline the many reasons why employers have increasingly sought to limit or even abandon long-established commitments to their employees. The outcome of such trends is the rise – or resurgence – of "*non*-standard" or "contingent" forms of employment: the hiring of temporary or part-time workers in lieu of permanent or full-time employees; the redefinition of workers (truck drivers, delivery people, technical personnel) as independent contractors; the use of out-sourcing or the off-shoring of work; expansive use of unpaid interns, and so forth. These new forms of employment have crucial effects on workers' lives, since they carry with them dramatic consequences for the provision of wages, job security, health insurance, sick days, and eligibility for retirement benefits (Kalleberg, Reskin, and Hudson, 2000; Kalleberg 2009). Workers in contingent positions often encounter subtle (and not-so-subtle) forms of harassment and marginalization, and firms find it increasingly possible to side-step legal obligations regarding wages and working hours, a phenomenon that Annette Bernhardt and her colleagues (2008) have termed the advent of the "gloves-off economy." And even for workers who remain stably employed, the trend toward casualization and the consequent fear of downward mobility have cut deep into the sinews of workplace life, compelling many workers to be more careful about what they say, think, and do. A "performative" quality may begin to creep into workplace life generally, in which workers grow more conscious of the need to maintain an energetic and dutiful appearance at all times. Employer controls over workers' identities, as discussed in this chapter, may grow that much more effective under such conditions of labor-market austerity (Smith 2010; Padavic 2005).

A third, and perhaps less well-understood, tendency gripping the advanced capitalist labor process is the "financialization" of work. This term has three distinct meanings, all of which leave their mark on the nature of work. First, there is the expansion of employment within occupations and industries involving financial analysis – for example, in commercial banks, the handling of stock portfolios, venture capital funds, insurance in all its different forms, real estate and other investments, currency exchanges, and risk management, and work of this sort. The expansion of these occupations (they have attracted a growing proportion of college graduates, especially in elite circles) signals an important shift in attitudes toward work generally. Second, there is the increasingly central role that financial activities play in control over a given nation's wealth. Because of the global prominence and power of financial institutions, a growing proportion of the GDP of the advanced capitalist nations has flowed into these firms, with consequences that have been felt with particular acuity in recent years.

It is the third meaning of "financialization" that commands our attention here. In this meaning of the term, I have in mind the increasing dominance of managerial conceptions that view work organizations solely in terms of their contributions to shareholder value. This conception of the firm has been gaining force within US capitalism since the early 1980s (see Useem 1996; Fligstein 2001), with the rising power of large institutional investors. Its relevance goes well beyond the pressure it imposes on executives to downsize their firms, or to pursue plant shutdowns or debt-fueled mergers and acquisitions. In addition, the financialization of work also implies an infusion of the financial model into the innermost recesses of workplace life in any number of industries – a process that has been shown to magnify previously existing inequalities (Tomaskovic-Devey and Lin, forthcoming).

Financialization in this sense has perhaps most carefully

been studied by the Minnesota anthropologist Karen Ho (2009a, b), who conducted participant observation at prominent Wall Street investment banks. Hired as a financial analyst, she encountered not only a dense workplace culture centered on the sanctity of shareholder value, but also a conception of work relations "that helps to construct insecurity as a normative, accepted feature of [workers'] lives, and that spurs them to spread this model of employee liquidity toward corporate America" (2009a: 185). By liquidity, Ho means not only wealth that can be easily moved or invested, but also the newly pliant nature of the Wall Street workers themselves – that is, their willingness to do whatever the market seems to demand of them, and to supply an "immediate responsiveness and an ability to constantly change direction and strategy." Referring to the investment banks she studied, Ho concludes that "their corporate culture creates a constant flow of interchangeable workers that permits banks to turn on a dime, as the only 'things' to shift are people who fully expect this instability" – and who even define it as a source of energy, pride, and invigoration (see 2009a: 186–7).

To be sure, the spread of this model of workplace life has been arrested by the economic crisis that began in 2007. Yet, ironically, the crisis may only deepen its grip on these employees, calling attention to the dangers, risks, and the latent power that the members of this strange tribe command. Implied here is a broader suggestion, implied in Ho's study, that these work settings may not be so exceptional as they might seem; and that they prefigure, in an unusually condensed and perhaps caricatured form, normative ensembles that gain purchase on workplace life well beyond Wall Street as such.

These arguments are sobering. They point again to forces that act to heighten employers' claims over workers' very identities. But they compel us to pose questions about the limitations that can inhere within overly deterministic models of work. For, arguably, many of the newer, culturally invested theories of labor control have committed many of the same sins and fallacies as did Braverman himself. To be sure, Hochschild's analysis of emotional labor has been chided in this way, for in the view of two British sociologists, her approach ignores the "potential for unmanaged spaces where 'moments of truth' may occur" (Bolton and Boyd 2003: 303). Surely the same charge – that of reifying capital's capacity to regulate workplace life – can be leveled at du Gay's analysis of the "enterprising self," and any effort to generalize Ho's argument beyond the confines of Wall Street as such. The point, discussed further in the next chapter, hinges on the need to acknowledge that social conditions not only limit, but also promote, the workers' capacity to renegotiate or resist the forms of control they currently face. Erving Goffman was right to observe that "every religious ceremony creates the possibility of a black mass" (1967: 86). No regime is ever fully effective; all produce "unmanaged spaces" which can sometimes be knitted together in ways that can have material effects.

3
From Fordism to Flexibility?

The last quarter of the twentieth century began a period of great economic flux and uncertainty throughout the Western capitalist world. The USA in particular experienced a series of wrenching changes, beginning with the energy crises and stagflation of the 1970s and the onset of sharp global competition and de-industrialization in the 1980s. With the advent of the technology-fueled "new economy" of the 1990s, it became clear to many that the economic ground was rapidly shifting underneath our feet. The argument became a mantra among management theorists: just as Britain had faced profound structural upheavals with the onset of the Industrial Revolution in the late eighteenth century, so too did the advanced capitalist nations face an era of rapid and profound structural change that was sure to have far-reaching consequences. Lofty claims, indeed – all the more so since they stemmed not only from academic circles, but also from analysts and decision-makers firmly ensconced in the corporate and public policy worlds.

Perhaps no single word has occupied a more central place in the ensuing debate than the concept of workplace flexibility. Inscribed on the banner of a movement with roots in many countries, the concept of flexibility has been at the heart of theory, research, and public policies across much of the Western world. Perhaps the most essential tenet in this discourse of flexibility has been a simple claim: the old regime of work, steeped in the bureaucratic "Fordist" model of mass production, has taken its final breaths. Supplanting it is a new, more fluid logic of work organization that promises to free workers from the disciplining structures of the past. These changes are said to operate at many levels. Workers will find themselves employed in autonomous teams, with greater responsibility than in the past. Firms will no longer operate in isolation or simple competition with one another; instead, they will embed themselves in complex webs of networks that, although often spatially proximate to one another, will participate in the global economy. Finally, advocates of this change forewarn, those nations that embrace the age of flexibility are the ones likely to succeed in the twenty-first century. Those who cling to the old Fordist model do so at their own peril.

Or so the argument goes. It is an argument that has massive implications, for it has bearing not only on global economic strategy and economic policy, but also on the claims that we can reasonably make of our jobs and our employers in the contemporary era. What will work come to mean in the twenty-first century? Will the notion of the career (in the sense of an orderly, predictable occupational trajectory) come to seem quaint? What institutions will anchor social life in the coming decades? Given such high stakes, the concept of flexibility has understandably provoked sharp debate (and, at times, militant social protest). Critics of workplace flexibility often dismiss this notion as little more than an ideological cover for the dismantling of job security and workers' rights; advocates point to the emergence of entirely new structures that represent viable and meaningful responses to the rise of global competition. In this chapter, I will argue that there is an element of truth in both of these positions.

The chapter begins with a critical analysis of one of the most influential strands of theory and research in this field – that based on the concept of "flexible specialization." Initially formulated by Piore and Sabel, this notion has gained an avid following among economic geographers, historians, social network theorists, and specialists in urban and regional planning. When we subject this literature to critical scrutiny, however, we begin to see several significant omissions in its argument. Yet rather than dismissing the concept of flexibility as a merely ideological construct – a latter-day equivalent of the concept of "progress," which disarmed the critics of industrial capitalism during the nineteenth century – I suggest that flexibility is a real, material development. To oppose it as such is to abandon the playing field to employers, who will shape the new labor regimes in accordance with their needs. Especially as the Fordist system of permanent employment encompasses a dwindling proportion of the labor force, the point may be to engage the new regimes, to shape them in ways to protect workers from their more damaging forms – in short, to "make flexibility work for labor" (Lash and Urry 1987: 282–3). There is a danger in doing so, of course: absent institutional supports, flexible systems of employment augur a new and more pernicious system of labor control than existed under Fordism. But that is precisely the point. If capitalism has entered a new and less rigidly organized stage in its development, and it therefore proves impossible to restore the logic of Fordist organizations, it will be crucial to ensure that institutional supports *are* present. By blunting their more coercive or neo-liberal features, we may even find it possible to institutionalize a freer and more fulfilling form of employment than Fordism allowed (Block 1990; Beck 2000).

The End of Fordism

One of the most widely influential studies of work that has appeared in the last quarter-century was Michael Piore and Charles Sabel's *The Second Industrial Divide* (1984). Written by an economist and a political scientist, this study constructed a bold comparative analysis of the model of work organizations that served as the engine of capitalist development throughout Western Europe, the United States, and Japan.

Piore and Sabel see economic development as periodically marked by key branching points, or "industrial divides." The *first* such divide occurred at the end of the nineteenth century, as the culmination of a struggle that had long been under way between two competing conceptions of work, or "technological paradigms." One – the mass production, or "Fordist" paradigm – is now highly familiar to us. As suggested, this is the large, highly centralized model of bureaucratic organization, in which large industrial corporations adopt a "low trust" model of work organization: workers are accorded little or no autonomy with respect to the method or pace of their work. Equally important, the Fordist model uses highly specialized, single-purpose tools and equipment to churn out large quantities of the same product. Because such an approach must devote substantial resources to highly rigid technologies, it typically makes sense only where there is extensive demand for standardized goods. This is why Adam Smith once wrote that "the division of labor . . . is limited by the extent of the market" (Smith 1939 [1776]: 17). Where the market for mass-produced goods is large and growing, Smith reasoned, employers will be compelled to adopt a sharply subdivided structure of work that would not be wise in other circumstances.

We are accustomed to view the Fordist paradigm as the logical culmination of modern production processes – that is, as the "end" toward which modern industry inevitably moved. What Piore and Sabel contend, however, is that the triumph of Fordism was not a matter of destiny or inevitability, but of arbitrary social processes that simply overwhelmed all alternatives. Most important here is the *second* technological paradigm they identify – craft production. This second paradigm typically involves small firms that embrace a "high trust" conception of work, in which skilled workers utilize general-purpose tools to produce specialty goods. While we are accustomed to viewing the craft paradigm as a sign of economic backwardness, Piore and Sabel find that, in fact, the craft paradigm provided the basis for a pattern of vibrant economic growth within what the British economist Alfred Marshall called "industrial districts." Here, in regions scattered throughout England, France, Germany, and Italy during the nineteenth century, small firms developed in close proximity to one another, making use of locally based expertise in the production of a single major product (e.g., specialty metals, shoes, woolen garments, textiles, cutlery, shipbuilding, ceramics, foodstuffs, and machinery of all types). The craft paradigm was one in which it was not the *firm* that sought to dominate a given industry, but rather a network of small firms all located within a particular *region*, where the "secrets of industry are in the air," as Marshall famously put it. Here, with municipal policies that provided stability within local industries, workers and their families could gain a steady and secure living without recourse to the rigid, centralized model that Fordism involved.

Why then did Fordism prevail? According to Piore and Sabel, the triumph of Fordism was due to a wholly arbitrary set of institutional influences that were most pervasively found in the United States. Three were especially important: the absence of a guild tradition, the malleability of American tastes, and the scarcity of skilled labor. These conditions proved highly favorable to the Fordist paradigm, for they provided the cultural ground in which demand for mass-produced goods could take root. These conditions – a huge potential market that was relatively homogeneous in cultural terms, open to consumption of mass-consumer goods, and equipped with unlimited supplies of unskilled immigrant workers – were highly conducive to the Fordist paradigm. While Europe was consumed with military struggles and divisions, Fordism was left to triumph and develop on the American terrain. Once it rose to economic dominance on the world stage, it was soon emulated by large enterprises in both Europe and Japan, enabling the mass-production paradigm to define itself as the reigning symbol of industrial modernity. The other side of this coin was that economic history was rewritten from the perspective of the victors – that is, from the point of view of the Fordist paradigm. Craft production came to be viewed largely in terms of its limitations – that is, as a symbol of economic irrationality and inefficiency. Perhaps the most significant monument to the logic of Fordism was the River Rouge plant, the largest plant in the world – and an industrial complex that was so vertically integrated that it contained its own steel-making and glass-making mills, in addition to automobile assembly.

Ordinarily, the Piore and Sabel analysis would be a matter of academic debate among economic and labor historians. But these are not ordinary times. To see their argument in such narrow terms would be both misleading and shortsighted. The reason is that the conditions that promoted and sustained the Fordist paradigm have now largely disappeared, leaving us a second branching point in modern economic development – the "second industrial divide" of the authors' title. Ironically, the very virtues that the craft paradigm provided are likely to enjoy newfound relevance in the contemporary economic landscape.

Piore and Sabel's argument identifies three reasons that serve to undermine the viability of the Fordist paradigm. First, as the capitalist economies have grown more interconnected with the global economy, the structures that previously served to maintain high levels of demand – those of Keynesian policies, in which national governments adjusted spending, thus stabilizing consumer markets – are no longer as effective as before. Thus, when the federal government increases its provisions for unemployment insurance, or adjusts federal spending to maintain aggregate demand, the result increasingly benefits foreign and not domestic producers. Especially given the limits of Keynesian policies, domestic producers using the Fordist paradigm are often ill-equipped to respond when economic downturns occur. Sharp fluctuations in demand confront them with chronic overcapacity and falling market shares. General Motors is the poster child of this affliction, government bailouts notwithstanding.

A second concern stems from the changing structure of consumer tastes. As mass-produced goods become virtually universal and demand for them reaches the saturation point, middle-class consumers in particular seek to distance themselves from such standardized goods. In other words, consumer preferences begin to shift in the direction of demand for quality goods – articles that enable consumers to symbolize their distinctive tastes (cf. Bourdieu 1984; Brubaker 1985). Consumer markets become more volatile, product cycles change more rapidly, and the key to survival in many industries hinges on the firm's ability to respond immediately to shifts in market demands. This provides a powerful incentive to avoid investing in rigid infrastructures, technologies, or systems of vertical integration – the very hallmarks of Fordist hierarchies.

A third development stems from the widespread diffusion of sophisticated information technologies, which makes it easier for manufacturers to engage in the production of quality "niche" commodities. Whereas before, entry into such markets was prohibitively expensive, requiring large amounts of capital, now computer-controlled equipment is within the reach of even small producers, who can turn out small batches of products in accordance with consumer tastes. Indeed, small producers find it increasingly possible to retool their production processes in accordance with local tastes – and to develop demand for their products precisely because of their nimble response to product cycles.

Given these conditions, a new technological paradigm – "flexible specialization" – is coming into view. It arises from two different vectors (Sabel 1982; Sabel et al. 1989). On the one hand, small firms have begun to form locally based networks that provide them with precisely those resources that were previously enjoyed only by large corporations – research and development, job training, and financial credit needed to foster investment – much of it orchestrated by local and state municipal programs that aim to foster the growth of small and medium-sized enterprises. On the other hand, large firms have increasingly sought to empower their own product divisions, seeking to "recreate among their subsidiaries and subcontractors the collaborative relationships" which smaller firms have historically enjoyed (Hirst and Zeitlin 1991: 4). The result is that the most economically vibrant industries and regions converge, using much the same flexible model of work organization. They abandon the rigid technologies and "low-trust" structures that defined the Fordist model of work organization, instead embracing a model that relies on the skills and initiative of skilled employees using multipurpose tools and equipment. Spatial proximity becomes important, as is seen in the tendency of many high-technology industries to cluster together in the same locale, where skilled workers come to establish occupationally rooted subcultures ("epistemic communities") that provide strategic resources for many industries (Hakanson 2005).

Three vital changes occur as a result. First, skilled workers begin to encounter greater residues of freedom and centrality within the firm than under the old Fordist paradigm. Second, organizational structures begin to shift, providing the advantage to smaller and more decentralized establishments that can respond to the flux and uncertainty of market trends. Finally, the boundaries among competing firms begin to blur, as collaborative networks arise that link firms to one another within the new industrial districts. Competition is increasingly overlaid with patterns of collaboration, as firms engage in subcontracting arrangements, partnerships, and strategic alliances with one another. In this way, they find it possible to avoid the risks of vertical integration, accomplishing through network embeddedness what they previously conducted in-house. As the last decade of the twentieth century unfolded, Hirst and Zeitlin were sufficiently enthused as to anticipate the "displacement of mass production by flexible specialization as the dominant technological paradigm of the late twentieth century" and beyond (1991: 36).

Flexible Specialization

Piore and Sabel initially formulated their theory in response to events that unfolded in North-Central Italy – most notably, in the Emilia-Romagna district. There, beginning in the late 1950s, a pattern of economic growth took root that was distinct from either the large industry that characterized Italy's northern cities, or the agricultural production in the nation's south. Dubbed "the Third Italy," by the 1980s the Emilia-Romagna district had achieved the lowest levels of unemployment and highest rates of productivity growth of any region in Italy. Once a relatively closed region that produced only for local consumption, by the 1970s the Emilian economy accounted for a disproportionately large share of Italy's exports of both consumer and producer goods, with especially large sales of knitwear, ceramics, leather goods, shoes, motorcycles, automatic machinery, and machine tools. The reason, Piore and Sabel argued, lay in the "Emilian model," in which small enterprises established strong collaborative relationships throughout the region, undergirding a significant presence nationally and internationally (Brusco 1982; Rinaldi 2005).

If the Emilian model had been confined to the "Third Italy," it would surely not have received the widespread attention it eventually enjoyed. Yet, as Piore and Sabel stressed, similar developments had emerged independently within industrial districts in other parts of Europe: the Baden-Württemberg region of Germany, one of the most advanced manufacturing centers in Western Europe; the Route 128 region of Cambridge, Massachusetts, now a vital cluster of biotechnology firms; and Silicon Valley in California. Since their book appeared, the list of such industrial districts has only grown, and now includes globally prominent clusters in various parts of India (especially in Hyderabad), China (including the high-tech clusters in Beijing, Shanghai, and Hong Kong, and the mammoth manufacturing cluster in Guangdong province), as well as Taiwan, Singapore, and other parts of the world (see Whitford and Potter 2007). Efforts to understand these developments have built on the Piore and Sabel model, generating widespread theorizing and research among economists, economic geographers, and social scientists of various stripes.

Some scholars have identified instances of flexible specialization in counter-intuitive places, such as the US film industry, which anticipated changes that later engulfed other industries. And, indeed, there is compelling evidence that the evolution of movie-making in the United States has closely corresponded to the Piore-Sabel model, tracing a path from Fordist mass production to flexible specialization (Storper 1994; see also Christopherson and Storper 1989). When the film industry took root in Los Angeles during the 1920s, films "were sold by the foot rather than on the basis of content," and the leading studios kept large staffs of writers, performers, and production personnel on their payrolls. They were expected to churn out as many as three or four films per week (Storper 1994: 201). Immediately following World War II, however, the vertically integrated, Fordist structure of the film industry was rapidly undermined by two developments – an anti-trust ruling from the US Supreme Court (which broke up studio ownership of cinemas) and the spread of television (which came to control the mass market for entertainment). By the late 1960s, the studios no longer relied on their own employees for set construction, lighting, make-up, or sound editing; instead, they subcontracted the work to small firms that specialized in these facets of film production. Studios became more like institutional investors, and script-writing and acting came under the control of independent film companies. Movie-making became project-driven, as studios and production companies established film-specific partnerships.[1]

Arguably, this whole history is likely to be repeated now in other media industries, such as print journalism, book and magazine publishing, and mainstream news outlets, which find their own Fordist structures besieged by the growth of the Internet, the blogosphere, and digital media generally.

Yet the central thrust of research on post-Fordist work structures has concerned not media, but such high-tech, knowledge-intensive industries as computer or software design, electronics, semi-conductors, automated machine-tool systems, and biotechnology. Here, research by the Berkeley geographer Annalee Saxenian is a case in point. In her *Regional Advantage* (1994), Saxenian compared two high-tech economic regions: the Route 128 corridor in Massachussetts and the Silicon Valley region around Palo Alto and the San Francisco Bay area. Building on their proximity to major research universities, both regions were powerhouses during the early days of the computer revolution. Yet, of these two regions, only Silicon Valley learned to adapt to competitive pressures from Japanese firms and maintained its global dominance. Saxenian asks why this outcome occurred.

Her answer is outlined in table 3.1. Saxenian introduces the concept "industrial system" to refer to the cultural norms and organizational structures that govern or inform the production systems in a given locale (the term is analogous to Piore and Sabel's concept of technological paradigm). The industrial system that predominated in the Route 128 corridor encouraged firms to operate at arm's length from one another, and to adopt vertically integrated structures for their key resources. By contrast, Silicon Valley's industrial system led firms to become embedded within dense networks of collaborative activity within the local region. Likewise, while Route 128's industrial system expected employees to be loyal to the corporate parent and to avoid taking risks, Silicon Valley's firms fostered patterns of mobility across firms, leading scientists and engineers to establish social networks that served as conduits of strategically important knowledge and information. These differences had material consequences. Route 128's industrial system was so rigid that when market conditions and consumer demand changed in rapid and unpredictable ways, the region's firms were unable

Table 3.1 Saxenian's theory of industrial systems and regional economic development

Dimension	Region	
	Silicon Valley	*Route 128*
Type of industrial system:	Decentralized, regional network-based	Independent, firm-based
Management style:	Loose, informal, egalitarian	Tight, formal, hierarchical
View of risk-taking, mobility:	Encouraged – failure as a badge of experience	Discouraged – mobility as betrayal
Sharing of knowledge:	Constant, even across firm boundaries, owing to strong occupational communities	Rare – proprietary view adopted
Integration vs alliances:	Vertical integration avoided; alliances constantly sought	Vertical integration as norm
Access to cutting-edge knowledge:	High, because of flexible ties to multiple constituencies	Low, because tethered to investments in older knowledge
Response to challenges of the 1980s:	Bets on mass production of memory chips. Falters, then recovers and leads in the production of PCs, software, processors	Bets on mini-computer market. Stumbles and fails to regain momentum

to respond. By contrast, Silicon Valley's firms proved to be substantially more resilient, weathered the new competition from Japan, and proved far better equipped to thrive in an uncertain world.

Central to Saxenian's argument, and to that of Piore and Sabel as well, are the pressures that emerge within the firm's environment. The notion is that when environments become too volatile, unpredictable, or complex for even large firms to control, firms must steadfastly avoid relying on vertically integrated structures. This is precisely the conclusion that emerges from a decade's worth of research by the Stanford sociologist Walter Powell and his colleagues, who have closely studied network ties established within the biotechnology industry (Powell, Koput, and Smith-Doerr 1996; Powell et al. 2005).

Put in the broadest terms, this industry has challenged the previously unrivaled position of big pharma – the large pharmaceutical firms that once dominated drug discovery – as spatially agglomerated clusters of small biotechnology firms have become important engines of regional economic development. Scrutinizing the network ties reported among US biotechnology firms, Powell and his colleagues find that the success of these firms depends on their ability to form multistranded relationships with other firms in regional networks: the greater the number of network ties a firm establishes, the more central its position within the network, and the greater its access to strategically important knowledge and scientific techniques. This in turn dramatically enhances its prospects of subsequent growth. As Powell later put it, "a firm grows by becoming a player; it does not become a player by growing" (2001: 60). Interestingly, the economic sociologist Brian Uzzi (1997) finds a similar pattern with respect to the New York apparel industry, which also faces a highly dynamic environment that is difficult to predict.

In later work, Powell (2001) has sketched the outlines of the new economic landscape, describing it in terms of "decentralized capitalism." Building on much of this literature, he argues that the twenty-first-century firm is marked by three important characteristics. First, the logic used to organize work is no longer based on the "job" but rather on the "project." Individual workers will no longer be expected to perform fixed and unchanging bundles of given tasks. Instead, firms will combine workers in heterogeneous teams whose composition constantly shifts from assignment to assignment. Projects are of relatively short duration and involve diverse sets of skills, compelling workers to engage in ongoing learning if they are to succeed. Second, Powell sees a generalized movement from hierarchies to networks as the basic unit of economic action. This shift is less pronounced in older industries where the legacy of Fordism is more pronounced. But, as the new model of work becomes more prominent, even large, centralized firms experience pressure from the emerging model, and begin to provide their subsidiaries with greater legal and organizational autonomy. Third, Powell sees the firm as engaging in efforts at cross-fertilization, in which assets or innovations from one domain are brought to bear on other branches of the economy, yielding benefits that blur product markets and broaden the firm's capacity to grow.

Scrutinizing Workplace Flexibility

A large literature has by now emerged on flexible specialization and on the concept of flexibility more generally. One important point seems beyond dispute: despite much-publicized claims that new technologies (and global capitalism generally) have shattered spatial barriers – a process some have called "de-territorialization" – spatially concentrated production systems have persisted, providing important platforms for industrial growth in both the developed and the developing world. Moreover, there is evidence that spatial proximity does provide strategic advantages (see Cainelli and de Liso 2005; Chen 2009). Surveying this literature, Whitford and Potter (2007) conclude that the very process of globalization, which fragments production processes into ever-smaller components, actually encourages the spatial agglomeration of specialty producers in economic clusters scattered around the globe.

Yet important uncertainties remain. Is the applicability of the model limited to knowledge-intensive production, or to the production of high-quality, diversified goods? Or does its influence spread more generally over the advanced capitalist economies? And is the prevalence of the model driven by its efficiency advantages? Or are social, political, and cultural influences the more critical mechanisms diffusing the new model across the advanced economies? These are important questions, to be sure. But of greater significance for our purposes here are the highly critical readings that flexibility theory has received in many quarters, which have raised far-reaching questions about the theory's validity.

Some analysts, such as the British scholar Anna Pollert (1991), see flexibility theory as relying on simplistic dichotomies that greatly distort the complexities and contradictions within economic institutions. She points out that even the Emilian model, long held up as an idealized model of the

virtues of flexibility, has often consigned substantial proportions of its labor force to the "black economy" (involving
informal and unregulated work; see Brusco 1982). In Pollert's
view, flexibility theory, now in vogue, has in fact "long since
passed its sell-by date." Others contend that the evidence
often used in support of the theory's claims embodies strong
selection biases. Since researchers tend to fasten on the most
beneficial cases, they have in effect invoked a "methodology
of exemplars" (Penn and Sleightholme 1995) that produces
an array of organizational "just-so stories" (Sewell 1995).

Out of the ferment that has emerged in the debate over
flexibility, three interrelated questions assume particular
importance. One centers on the actual shape, or contours, of
the new production networks, and the degree to which they
signify meaningful shifts with respect to the distribution of
economic power. A second involves the ways in which flexible work regimes alter the position of the front-line worker
in the advanced capitalist nations. The third and perhaps
most important question of all is whether the advent of flexible work organizations represents the rise of a new form
of labor control, or instead an engine of economic growth
that is capable (and worthy) of generating widespread public
support.

The shape of flexible networks

The first of these questions is most frontally addressed in
an important work by the late economist Bennett Harrison
– *Lean and Mean: The Changing Landscape of Corporate
Power in an Age of Flexibility* (1994). In this book, the author
develops a number of important points. First, he views the
distinction between Fordism and flexibility as misleading in
many respects. Large Fordist firms can achieve flexible modes
of operation in many ways without abandoning their deeply
hierarchical logic of organization. This is true, for example,
when firms use software-controlled production systems that
can retool their product lines with little or no down-time
(a phenomenon that some have called "flexible Fordism").
Second, Harrison argues that the flexibility literature has
tended to fasten one-sidedly on the benevolent facets of the

new economic clusters, looking only at employees who have remained with the "core" of these new structures. Employees whose work has been externalized, or repositioned organizationally or spatially, are seldom given much consideration.

The key argument Harrison develops, however, concerns the actual contours of the new production systems, which he describes as involving "concentration without centralization." By this term he means a structural pattern through which large corporations can retain their disproportionate economic power by establishing webs of supply chains in lieu of the old pattern of vertical integration. Large firms continue to hold positions of centrality within each network, now without the fixed obligations that ownership had involved. As Harrison puts it:

> Rather than dwindling away, concentrated economic power is changing its shape, as the big firms create all manner of networks, alliances, short and long-term financial and technology deals – with one another, with governments at all levels, and with legions of generally (though not invariably) smaller firms who act as their suppliers and subcontractors. (1994: 8)

He therefore speaks of the proliferation of decentralized production units, but in relationships that leave small firms beholden to the concentrated power of the very largest firms in the network. What results, then, is "geographically and organizationally dispersed production," often in ways that agglomerate within particular regions, "but with strategy, marketing, and finance ultimately controlled by" the large firms at the center of the network (ibid.: 22).

The virtue of Harrison's book lies in its insistence on scrutinizing the structure of the new production networks, and in its recognition that there are many ways through which large corporations can gain the flexibility they require. His thinking suggests, for example, that production networks and supply chains can assume a variety of forms, some of which bear little resemblance to the symmetrical or collaborative relations so often viewed as the essential attributes of the flexible firm. In fact, the corporate quest for flexibility may more commonly lead firms within the developed world to resort to the deeply asymmetrical models used by retail chains selling designer goods.

This very argument has been advanced by analysts concerned with global commodity chains, who speak of a broad structural shift in the structure of supply chains characteristic of the post-Fordist era. Previously, when capital-intensive manufacturing firms predominated, "producer-driven" commodity chains were prevalent, in which large industrial corporations controlled their suppliers and retailers. Now, "buyer-driven" commodity chains have emerged in which large retailers and big-box stores such as Walmart, The Gap, The Limited, Benetton, or Banana Republic occupy the most powerful nodes in any given commodity chain (Gereffi 1994, 2001; Bair 2005; Collins 2005). This is an important development, and one that represents a dramatic change from the Fordist era – but it hardly shifts the distribution of economic power in a more egalitarian direction.

Moreover, recent trends suggest that the advent of small, collaborative networks tends over time to give rise to giant contractors who come to hold dominant positions within global supply chains. This has happened to some extent in the Emilian case, but the trend is far more pronounced in the global apparel industry, as giant firms such as TAL, Luen Thai Holdings and Li and Fung have carved out new and highly powerful positions within apparel contracting (Appelbaum 2009; Bonacich and Wilson 2008: 28–33). These firms have grown so formidable as to provide a wide array of functions that were previously controlled by the big buyers. These garment contractors are capable of providing design, production, logistics, and even inventory management for large retailers, including the delivery of products directly to the buyer's stores, thus greatly speeding up product availability in an industry where fashion and speed are crucial. The growth of powerful contractors is also apparent in computers and electronics, where leading retailers like Dell, Apple, and HP all rely on such giant firms such as Foxconn for manufacturing, design, and supply-chain management. Foxconn is one of the global titans of electronics contracting but is itself owned by Hon Hai Group, the largest electronics contractor in the world (Barboza, "Clues in an iPhone Autopsy," *New York Times*, 6 July, 2010).

These observations have two important implications. First, while production networks do supplant large Fordist firms, the result can assume a wide array of forms, the most prominent of which seem likely to reproduce or even to deepen the stark inequalities that characterized the Fordist regime. And, second, as the firms within such hierarchical networks concentrate economic power, they gain an increasing ability to shape their environments, rather than passively responding to them (as so many organizational theorists assume). This last point has been made forcefully in a recent study by the Stanford organizational theorist Stephen Barley, who documents the ways in which large corporations have succeeded in wielding power over their political environments, constructing an organization field that has enveloped important legislative and regulatory apparatus within the federal government (2010).

Advent of the high-trust model?

A second question is how the shift toward flexible production networks reshapes the work situations of front-line workers in the advanced capitalist world. Here, much of the literature on workplace flexibility has portrayed the dismantling of Fordist structures as making possible certain emancipatory possibilities. In some versions of this argument, a series of bold and even heroic assumptions are made about the growing importance or centrality that workers come to enjoy in the post-Fordist world. This is the argument made by the German scholars Horst Kern and Michael Schuman (1992), who speak of the reintegration of mental and manual skills within leading German metalworking and machinery plants – a development that seemed to affirm Piore and Sabel's conception of a "neo-craft" model of workplace control. It is the argument advanced by the Harvard management theorist Shoshana Zuboff (1988), whose fieldwork led her to conclude that new information technologies cannot effectively be used in the context of highly centralized bureaucratic structures, and that newer "post-hierarchical" arrangements were likely to emerge that required workers to master a set of analytic or "intellective" skills that reversed the routinization that predominated under Fordist manufacturing. Most recently, a similar argument has been made in the work of the urban theorist Richard Florida (2003), whose *The Rise of the Creative Class* views workers in the arts, media, design, educational, and professional fields as forming a new and highly powerful class of creative specialists, whose cultivation is central to urban and regional growth, and who come to enjoy a freedom that no single employer could provide. In a somewhat different way, Daniel Pink, author of *Free Agent Nation* (2001), envisioned an era of emancipation as alternative forms of economic activity took root in a post-bureaucratic age. Perhaps the most empirically grounded study in this vein is Debra Osnowitz's (2011) *Freelancing Expertise*, which carefully documents the entrepreneurial subculture in which computer and editorial consultants are embedded.

Evaluating these claims leads one to a number of conclusions. First, it is certainly arguable that many of the more celebrated forms of corporate job redesign (High Performance Work Organizations, self-directed team systems, and other initiatives of this sort) have begun to shift work organizations in the direction that flexibility theory expects. There is no question that a growing proportion of large US corporations and establishments have indeed embraced such changes (see the discussions in Vallas 1999 and 2003a). The recent study by Jeremy Reynolds (2006) is representative. Using the second wave of the National Organizations Survey, he finds that a substantial minority of workers in the largest occupations – 47 per cent of skilled production workers, and 34 per cent of machine operators – now belong to teams that enjoy significant control over task assignments or work methods. Yet Reynolds also finds that team systems are generally developed with respect to work groups that *already have* valuable skills. That is, there is no evidence that employers tend to embrace a "high-trust" model with respect to less privileged workers, and thus no evidence of any enhancement effect. Moreover, in my own research in manufacturing settings (2003a, 2006), I find that successful implementation of team systems often rests on workers' ability to usurp the new forms of work organization, driving them in directions that managers would prefer to avoid.

Much more important than the diffusion of this or that program for worker empowerment or employee involvement, however, is the fact that so much of the research on flexible specialization and the post-Fordist regimes has tended to fixate on the *benefits* that flexible regimes provide, thus providing an idealized picture of flexible employment that systematically overlooks the often sobering *costs*, or what Harrison called "the dark side of flexibility." It bears remembering in this connection that small enterprises have consistently higher rates of mortality than do more established firms. They provide lower wages, fewer benefits, and much harsher conditions of employment. And larger firms in the process of seeking greater flexibility often adopt cost-cutting practices that exile large numbers of their employees into more peripheral positions, for example, by repositioning them within satellite firms, redefining employees as independent contractors, or otherwise relocating workers within far more precarious and poorly paid jobs. This point – essentially, that the new production networks are partly responsible for the resurgence of inequality, or the "new dualism" – has been raised by Harvey (1989), Atkinson (1985), and by Harrison himself.

A new system of labor control?

Implied in the above line of interrogation is an argument that was broached in the previous chapter, and that warrants serious consideration here: a growing number of scholars have responded to the theory of flexible specialization by developing an alternative theory under the rubric of "flexible accumulation" (see especially Rubin 1995, 1996; Harvey 1989; Lash and Urry 1987). This is more than a semantic repackaging, for it involves a sharply different conception of the emerging structures at work.

Flexible accumulation theorists acknowledge the bureaucracy-transcending impulses inherent in the new capitalism, part of a broader trend that the British scholars Scott Lash and John Urry (1987) call the "end of organized capitalism." But they see the result as congealing in a new labor regime that is able to use the condition of labor-market uncertainty as a lever with which to augment the firm's capacity to regulate its workers' behavior. In this view, the new regime is characterized by four key conditions: (1) a restless competitive struggle for control over markets and sources of revenue, rather than the collaborative or communitarian arrangements that Piore and Sabel foresaw; (2) boundary-heightening tendencies, widening the gulf between those who remain within the core of the firm and those who are exiled to its periphery (or even exiled to subcontractors outside the firm entirely); (3) the dismantling of many labor-market shelters and internal labor markets within the firm; and (4) a consequent empowerment of the corporation, although in ways that discard bureaucratic forms of work organization and supplant them with more organizational patterns that minimize the constraints on employers' practices.

In this view, varied occupations are drawn into the new regime, some of them from their very moment of development. This is the case with many workers in knowledge-intensive occupations – those who perform "immaterial labor" (or "cognitive capitalism"), as in the case of new media workers and web designers. Although such work is often glamorized as filled with self-determination (careers without boundaries, the heroes of "free agency," and so on), the bulk of such employees may well flit about from project to project without the ability to plan more than a few weeks or months in advance. As New York University cultural studies scholar Andrew Ross describes these work situations:

> [T]he condition of entry into the new high-stakes lottery is to leave your safety gear at the door; only the most spunky, agile and dauntless will prevail. This narrative is little more than a warmed-over version of social Darwinism, but, when phrased seductively, it is sufficiently appealing to those who are up for the game. Once they are in, some of the players thrive, but most subsist, neither as employers nor employees, in a limbo of uncertainty, juggling their options, massaging their contacts, never knowing where their next project or source of income is coming from. (2008: 36)

Commenting on the broader meaning of this trend, the social theorist Zygmunt Bauman observes that:

> Secure jobs in secure companies seem to be the yarn of grandfathers' nostalgia . . . Flexibility is the catchword of the day. It augurs jobs without in-built security, firm commitments

or future entitlements, offering no more than fixed-term or rolling contracts, dismissal without notice and no right to compensation. No one can therefore feel truly irreplaceable – neither those already outcast nor those relishing the job of casting others out. (2000: 161–2)

Drawing on Bauman's theory of "liquid modernity" (in which the solid attributes of industrial capitalism give way to lighter, softer, and more malleable structures that constitute the contemporary era), we might even term this new regime one of "liquid capitalism." For the argument here is that nothing is assured from moment to moment – and the resulting anxiety itself provides a lever with which the firm can not only exact compliance, but can also engage workers in competitive market relations as well.

In his own very different argument about "decentralized capitalism," Powell had rejected this argument. In his view, there was nothing intrinsic in the new network forms that involve the coercive, controlling elements sketched out above. Rather, Powell contends that harsh and unforgiving conditions certainly occur, but are an expression of the difficulties involved in the transition to a new logic of economic organization. Once the logic has been institutionalized and – as he fervently advocates – once the necessary governmental supports are in place, the risks and hardships associated with the new production systems will have largely faded away.

The difficulty with this argument is that precisely the opposite trends have been under way for some decades now. Indeed, there has been a widespread withdrawal of government protection of the right to join labor unions, declining support for unemployed workers, the privatization of much public employment, and the emergence of a far more punitive conception of poverty for nearly a generation. It therefore becomes increasingly difficult to view workplace flexibility in so innocuous a light as Powell recommends.

Yet, in one respect, his reasoning suggests an important point about the new regime: precisely because of its liquid, post-bureaucratic nature, it is "under-determined" to a significant degree. That is, it is not inherently structured in ways that operate to the disadvantage of labor. It is in theory quite capable of being reshaped in ways that better accord with workers' needs. Indeed, some of the government interventions Powell himself suggests would begin to move toward this end. Arguably, the question hinges on the social and political institutions that could be introduced to reframe the meaning of flexibility.

Ironically, to raise this question is to return to a theme that was emphasized at the very outset of the debate over flexible specialization but has since been neglected. Then, scholars were keenly aware that the successes of the Emilian model, for example, owed much to the active institutional support the industrial districts enjoyed from local and regional Social Democratic political parties. Such support stemmed from a coalition formed among manufacturing workers, small business owners, and agricultural producers, all of whom found virtue in the collective resources the Emilian region provided (credit for the establishment of new businesses, employment banks providing skills and technical education, and job security for workers in between positions). This was in fact why Charles Sabel's (1982) first book carried the title *Work and Politics,* and why he was skeptical of arguments rooted in the pursuit of efficiency. "The more you look at Italian developments," he concluded, "the more you are driven to conclude again that, within the broad limits imposed by competition in world markets, economic structure is fixed by political choices" (1982: 231). Perhaps, then, we are all Italian now.

What institutional systems could be devised to prevent the new production systems from congealing into a new and more pernicious system of labor control than Fordism itself? How might it be possible to avoid neo-liberal variants of flexible labor regimes, and instead foster more collaborative forms of flexibility? Some preliminary answers can be found in the social movements that have emerged in Western Europe within the last decade. Beginning in 2001, and apace with the development of the European Union, there emerged a surprising coalition of university students, union activists, migrant workers, artists, and workers in new media industries, who engaged in coordinated EuroMayDay demonstrations that began in Milan but eventually spread into Barcelona, Madrid, Paris, Rome, and other major cities throughout Western Europe, and became a politically significant force. Several points are of interest in this movement.

First and perhaps most important was the *object* of the movement. The rallying cry of this movement answered to many names – in French, *précarité*; in Italian, *incertezza* (or uncertainty); in German, *Unsicherheit* (insecurity). But the movement eventually targeted its protest actions against the post-Fordist condition participants came to call *precarity*, which one activist defined as "the condition of being unable to predict one's fate" or "to plan one's time . . . being a worker on call where your life and time are determined by external forces" (Foti 2004; Bodnar 2006; Ross 2008; LaVaque-Manty 2007). Refusing this liminal condition of permanent uncertainty, movement participants articulated a sense of indignation and solidarity that was prevalent among the workers in their ranks – temporary workers, the intermittently employed, those on fixed-term contracts or performing state-subsidized work ("one-euro-an-hour" jobs), as well as undocumented migrant workers. In so doing, the movement in effect appropriated the concept of flexibility and de-euphemized it; that is, it redefined it in more worker-centered terms that emphasized its structural deficiencies. Moreover, participants came to refer to themselves as representing a new subjectivity: the "precariat," playfully invoking Marx's proletariat.

Second and equally fascinating were the *tactics* that were employed in the anti-precarity movement. Drawing on their own creative skills and expertise, but turning them against their employers, web designers and other new media workers constructed a wide array of materials as the tools of their mobilization work – websites, zines, video clips, DVDs, listservs, "subvertisements" – and used them to establish transnational networks that by 2005 had a presence in 17 major European cities. One website created a digital platform called *Precarity Ping Pong*, through which activists openly shared information, played simulation games across cities, and posted cultural critiques of the "flexploitation" they encountered. Harkening back to the English Luddite movement, which invented the fictitious leader Ned Ludd nearly two centuries ago, activists in the Italian precarity movement created the fictitious San Precario, "the patron saint of precarious, casualized, sessional, intermittent, temporary, flexible, project, freelance and fractional workers" (see figure 3.1).

Figure 3.1 "San Precario," the fictitious patron saint of the precariously employed. Note the cell phone at his waist and the name tag on his shirt, signifying the precarious position of the chain worker in a dead-end, insecure job (see: <www.precaria.org>)

The saint appears in public spaces on occasions of rallies, marches, interventions, demonstrations, film festivals, fashion parades, and, being a saint, processions. Often he performs miracles ... Equitable in his choices, San Precario does not privilege one category of precarious worker over another, and he can appear in supermarkets in urban peripheries, in bookstores or, glammed up, at the Venice Film Festival. San Precario is also transgender, and it has appeared also as a female saint. A "cult" has spread rapidly.[2]

Interweaving serious political work with significant elements of play, activists framed their movement in alignment with the existing institutional framework (for example, religion), in a largely successful effort to bring public attention and sympathy to their cause.

Perhaps the most relevant feature of the movement for our purposes involved its *goals*. The movement invoked a radical discourse that was steeped in the work of Marx and Foucault. They expressed little sympathy for the "sclerotic" political parties and trade unions they perceived, and preferred to engage in direct action tactics. Yet, in many respects, the movement embraced a program that involved relatively moderate transitional reforms. References were commonly made to the program of "flexicurity," a system of labor laws and social insurance provisions that protected Dutch and Danish workers from the worst forms of abuse, and which activists wanted strengthened and applied throughout the entirety of the EU. The movement's leaders made plain their rejection of the Fordist employment relation, and their wish to retain certain features of post-Fordist production systems. Said one of the most influential activists, Alex Foti, expressing his view of creative or "immaterial" labor:

> in one sense flexicurity means we do not want to go back to a "job for life" – the system of the previous generation. We accept the flexibility inherent in the computer-based mode of production, but we want to disassociate from the precarity that is implicit in this forced, Faustian bargain. (Foti 2004: 2)

The point here is that the movement of the self-styled precariat rejected the neo-liberal formulation of post-Fordist arrangements, but in a way that sought to preserve the self-determination that flexibility could provide.

This movement very likely reached its culmination in the spring of 2006 in France, when it mobilized a massive series of protests that managed to block the implementation of labor-market measures that would have weakened the position of French youth (Bennhold, *New York Times*, April 11, 2006). Whether recent economic developments will favor the movement's resurrection is far from clear. Nor is it easy to imagine an equivalent movement arising in the contemporary United States. Still, several points emerge from this brief discussion.

First, the precarity movement stands as an example of a broadly based effort to redefine the meaning of workplace flexibility, now in accordance with the workers' own needs. It stands as an action-critique of the new flexible work regimes. As such, it begins to point toward viable reforms that glean what is emancipatory within the new production systems, while eliminating their most coercive or degrading aspects. Precisely what policies might be suggested along these lines – an American equivalent of flexicurity – seems less important than the urgency of the need to implement them in one form or another. Implied here is a lesson that speaks to much of the literature discussed throughout this chapter: the promise immanent within the concept of workplace flexibility is not entirely illusory. Nor can it be ignored. Realizing the possibilities latent within the new production systems will require more than the vagaries of the marketplace alone can provide (Neilson and Rossiter 2008).

4

Ascriptive Inequalities at Work, I: Gender

It is a sad but useful puzzle. Imagine a father and son on their way to a sports event. On the way, their automobile is struck by another vehicle. Both father and son are seriously hurt, and the son's injuries are so severe as to warrant emergency surgery to save his life. Yet when the boy is wheeled into the operating room, the surgeon looks down in dismay, and cries out: "I can't operate on this patient. This is my son!"

How can this paradox be explained? Students often wrestle with this question, tying themselves into logical or factual knots. Was the surgeon merely the biological father? Did the father recover more fully from the accident than initially thought? Of course, the solution is both simple and disturbing: the surgeon was a woman – an obvious possibility that our culture has made it difficult for us to grasp.

The story demonstrates a point that is axiomatic among social scientists studying work: cultures often establish unspoken rules that come to govern the allocation of people into specific occupations. Certain types of work, in other words, are implicitly reserved for the members of particular groups. Such rules can govern entry into highly prestigious occupations (excluding those who can't look or act the part, quite apart from their actual abilities), as well as jobs that are held in low esteem (where workers of a given gender or race tend to be clustered). The point is that studying work requires that we explore not only the *structure* of work – its architecture, as explored in the preceding chapters. We must also explore the *allocation* of work – that is, the social and cultural processes that quietly act to define the appropriate types of people who "should" be channeled into particular jobs, occupations, and industries. These allocation-related processes have received substantial social-scientific attention in recent years, as social movements, legal institutions, and political forces have all combined to generate sharp and at times acrimonious debate over equal employment opportunity, disparities in pay, and questions regarding the access that women and minority employees enjoy as they seek full inclusion within the most rewarding occupations in our society. To address these questions is to embark on the study of ascriptive inequalities at work – that is, to examine how workers' membership in a given sex, race, or ethnic group impinges on the social relations they are likely to encounter at work, in turn affecting the distribution of employment opportunity within the firm and the economy as well.

In exploring this terrain, we do so by first discussing gender inequalities. Why have women remained so under-represented in the most powerful and well-rewarded occupations (as in the case of the surgeon, with whom this chapter began)? Why have gender inequalities proved so resilient and pervasive in spite of institutional and legal shifts that would seem to level the playing field? These questions provide the focus of the present chapter. Following it, our attention then shifts to the study of racial and ethnic disparities at work, exploring how jobs and labor markets have not only been gendered, but racialized as well.

Studying Gender Inequality at Work

The study of work and gender under capitalism has a long and venerable history, reaching back into debates that emerged at the very origin of the Industrial Revolution in the eighteenth century. Yet it was only in the years following World War II that systematic research began to appear on the social and institutional mechanisms that account for the subordinate positions women have come to hold within work organizations and the occupational structure generally. The timing of

this shift can hardly be viewed as accidental, for it was at precisely this moment – the decades that began with World War
II – when dramatic structural changes began to unfold in the
economic and social positions that women held. Beginning
in the 1950s especially, women's rates of labor-force participation grew exponentially. Women's levels of education
(including their enrollment in elite professional schools)
caught up with and began to surpass those of men. Both
reflecting and reinforcing these social trends, the federal government enacted civil rights legislation that mandated equal
employment opportunity for women (and racial minorities).
And with the availability of birth control and reproductive
rights generally, women found it possible to challenge deeply
held assumptions about their relation to paid labor, which
had long limited their employment opportunities. There
should be no mystery why many scholars have referred to
these changes as amounting to a gender revolution.

Yet, although there can be little debate that women have
made remarkable gains throughout the advanced capitalist
societies, gender inequality has proved to be a remarkably
tenacious phenomenon. For one thing, sex segregation at
work has remained deeply inscribed within the occupational
structure. Although there has been progress on this score,
with a decline in the level of occupational segregation by sex,
men and women typically hold very different jobs. Compare
the lists of the ten largest jobs held by men and by women,
and one finds few points of overlap. Men are still largely
found in historically male-dominated occupations such as
laborer, truck driver, and manager, while large numbers
of women can still be found in such heavily feminized jobs
as secretaries, elementary school teachers, and nurses. This
pattern of occupational segregation by sex is far more pronounced than its racial and ethnic equivalent.

And these differences are nearly always accompanied by
inequality and subordination. Indeed, although there has been
a narrowing of the gender gap in pay since 1970, and some
movement toward the integration of work along gender lines,
such trends have largely stalled (and in some cases reversed
directions) since the mid-1990s. Among year-round, full-time
workers over the age of 15, women earned only 77 cents for
every dollar paid to men in 2010. Partly reflecting women's

lower pay, and partly owing to the powerful stigma attached to "women's work," efforts to break down the sex-typing of jobs have usually involved the movement of women into male-dominated jobs, with little movement of men into feminized occupations. And although women now account for a substantial proportion of the student population in medical, law, and business schools, they remain remarkably underrepresented at the most senior or elite levels. The Federal Glass Ceiling Commission (1995) reported that women made up only 3 to 5 percent of the senior executives employed at Fortune 500 corporations in the mid-1990s. Sex segregation among managerial occupations has in fact tended to grow since then, and both male and female managers suffer lower salaries when they are employed in female-dominated fields (Cohen, Huffman, and Knauer 2009; Cotter et al. 2004).

Some questions thus arise. What are the social and historical roots of gender segregation at work? Why has gender inequality at work remained so prevalent and so resistant to change? Why have men continued to enjoy occupational privileges that are denied to women, even as gender disparities in education, labor-force participation, and levels of occupational commitment have all but withered away? What legal remedies have been adopted, and with what effects?

In addressing these questions, the chapter begins by providing a brief discussion of the historical emergence of gender inequality during the transition to industrial capitalism. It then explores five strands of theory and research that scholars have advanced in an effort to understand gender disparities at work. These strands of thought will also prove useful in the following chapter, involving racial and ethnic disparities.

The Gendering of Work in the United States

Viewed from one perspective, it should not be surprising that men and women continue to hold such different and unequal positions at work. For gender divisions have a long history that reaches back to the emergence of industrial capitalism itself. To say this is to confront several important and widely held myths about the position that women hold within paid employment. It is also to uncover the sources of many assumptions that continue to limit women's economic options today.

First, far from being newcomers to the sphere of production, women were in fact central players in the rise of the factory system. Women have always participated in productive activity, of course; only the most privileged of women could afford not to engage in economic activities. Thus the great bulk of the population in Europe and the United States relied on the coordinated labor of both women and men on farms and in home-based workshops. The household itself was the major unit of productive activity in pre-industrial society. Although men held the dominant positions, and patriarchal norms obliged women to submit to control by their husbands and fathers, women's work was vitally important to the well-being of the family and generally recognized as such. Especially in Puritan America, idleness was viewed as sinful; in a developing society with a labor shortage, each member of the community and household was expected to make an economic contribution. What the rise of industrial capitalism did was to dramatically transform these arrangements, instituting social and cultural norms that not only defined the nature of men's and women's work, but also shaped socially dominant conceptions of gender in ways that have continued to affect everyday life even today.

Initially, the rise of the factory system in the United States provided an expanding set of opportunities for men and women alike. Indeed, in the early decades of the nineteenth century, many employers were especially keen to hire women workers. Since their labor was less closely tethered to the rhythms of agrarian harvests, they were often deemed a more reliable source of labor than were men. As the Industrial Revolution gripped the Western economies, women became a significant proportion of the factory population, actually making up the the majority of the manufacturing population in mid-nineteenth-century America, often producing goods that had previously been made within the home, such as clothing, shoes, bread, soap, candles, and paper (see Kessler-Harris 1982: ch. 2). As work relentlessly migrated from the home to the factory, young women followed this migration, often viewing paid employment as providing important sources of independence and achievement.

Yet the specter of women engaged in industrial employment provoked a fateful public debate that grew quite heated during the first half of the nineteenth century, and ultimately generated a highly restricted conception of women's "place" as lying exclusively within the domestic sphere (Lerner 1969; Welter 1966; Kerber 1988). Where previously, women had been recognized and rewarded for engaging in economic activity, this period witnessed the emergence of a new conception of women that idealized women's feminine virtues, which were now defined as "naturally" finding their rightful expression only through domestic, family, and household pursuits. In this conception, paid employment was redefined as a moral transgression, a violation of the ideal of "True Womanhood" – or even of women's essential nature as such. This conception was advocated by a broad and diverse set of constituencies – civic and religious leaders, medical experts, leaders of elite women's organizations, and writers of women's literature and popular magazines – all of whom propounded a "cult of domesticity" that defined women's nature in terms of four central ideals: purity, piety, domesticity, and submissiveness. A broad, elite-driven cultural movement, this cult of domesticity idealized women's domestic roles as mothers, wives, and supporters of religious worship, and defined women as the keepers of the society's most sacred virtues and ideals, which had come under siege by the cruel and heartless logic that industrial capitalism had itself unleashed. In this changed cultural context, women who pursued paid employment were said to have abandoned their proper moral obligations, and to have acted in ways that violated a woman's delicate nature. Moreover, doing so not only invited moral rebuke: in addition, it risked physiological and medical ailments of various kinds. "Menstrual dysfunction, uterine disorders and insanity were said to result from overwork, routinized work, and certain body positions imposed" by wage labor, at least in the eyes of medical authorities (Kessler-Harris 1982: 106).

At least part of the reason why this broad cultural movement arose stems from the cultural strains that accompanied the rise of a newly affluent propertied class in early and mid-nineteenth-century America. As agrarian communities gave way to urban life, and as individual competition undermined the civic obligations that had secured the early republic, wealthy merchants and elites found it necessary to legitimate the newly emerging capitalist order in the eyes of the public. At the same time, affluent women needed to establish a legitimate role for themselves in an era when domestic production was increasingly superfluous. Under these conditions, it is understandable why the cult of domesticity would arise. By defining women's place as that of the keepers of civic and moral virtue, the cult of domesticity met the needs of these audiences, undergirding the legitimacy of the social order they sought to protect.

Clearly, the idealized image of the domestic wife and mother offered cold comfort to working-class, immigrant and minority women, whose earnings were often vital to the well-being of their families. And, indeed, there were expressions of protest against the cult of domesticity. In the 1830s, women sometimes pressed for improvements in the conditions of their employment, even striking for better wages. Yet doing so only invited public blame and recrimination, as the leading organs of public opinion dubbed such transgressions as threatening to install "Amazonian" traditions, or even a "gynocracy," on American shores (Kessler-Harris 1982: 43). Efforts to challenge the cult of domesticity also met with resistance from decidedly non-elite circles, as working men and their organizations increasingly formed a tacit alliance with elite merchants and the leaders of women's and religious organizations. Working men viewed the influx of women into paid employment as posing a significant threat, not only to their labor-market positions but also to their very identity as working men.[1]

Although men and women typically worked in separate industries, this was not always the case. In industries such as textiles and shoe-making, employers hired both men and women, but in sharply separate occupations: skilled work for men and less skilled work for women. The onset of mechanized equipment often disrupted these customary gender distinctions and enabled employers to hire women in place of men. Moreover, employers often had a strong incentive to do so, since women's wages were usually half those of their male counterparts, and since women were widely assumed to be more easily controlled than were men. As a consequence, working men often did find their labor-market position undercut by women workers, resulting in what an 1836 labor report called "ruinous competition." In theory, it might have been possible for men to form common cause with their sisters, wives, and daughters, acting on the basis of class solidarity. In practice, working men often acted in accordance not with a class-based logic but with the logic of gender uppermost in mind, thus viewing the hiring of women workers as a source of their emasculation. In various industries, working men agitated not for women's rights to a decent wage, but to the man's right to a wage that was sufficient to keep his wife at home. In effect, workers signed on to the cult of domesticity, embracing this elite-spawned doctrine and claiming an equal right to benefit from a male-dominated economy.

This "cult of domesticity" had pernicious effects that have endured from that day to this. For one thing, until well after World War II, it was widely assumed that only young or unmarried women would enter the sphere of paid employment. Employers commonly expected women to resign once they married, and often strictly enforced this norm as company policy (Cohn 1985). If a woman continued to work after marriage (let alone childbirth), that was viewed as an indication that something had gone awry: the death, disability, or desertion of the husband, for example. The implication, then, was that women were mere migrants, temporarily granted rights to occupy the terrain of paid employment.

A corollary of this development was that the meaning of a woman's activities within the home was sharply redefined: no longer were these viewed as "work"; now, this term acquired a more specific meaning. "Real" work was limited to activities undertaken for a wage or salary, within the paid labor force. The woman's activities as homemaker, care giver, cook, and cleaner were therefore absorbed into the ambiguous category of "non-work," since their labor here is provided without the litmus test of "work" – the wage (Reskin and Padavic 2003: 23). The rise of industrial capitalism thus signaled a widening disparity in the power and recognition accorded to men's and women's economic activity.

Perhaps the most significant consequence of this redefinition of gender and work, however, lay in its tendency to "naturalize" the socially constructed image of women as frail and delicate creatures best suited for care-giving and nurturing activities. This notion, which for generations has claimed to capture women's essential or "natural" traits, left an enduring mark on the employment opportunities that women have been able to pursue and on the occupational structure writ large. Although we tend to assume that the sex-typing of work reflects men's and women's inherent traits, in fact the most prevalent patterns of occupational segregation were only recently established. Up until the Civil War years, for example, the jobs of telephone operators, secretaries, clerks, and stenographers were all overwhelmingly male occupations. It was not until the rise of industrial capitalism and the expansion of routine office labor that the lower ranks of office employment came to be feminized. Likewise, after a period in which male apprentices were employed as switchboard operators, AT&T rapidly feminized the ranks of the operators in the 1890s. Its success was so convincing that later company memoranda mocked the earlier effort to employ men as operators, since these jobs were "obviously" women's work (Vallas 1993). At the same time, the period 1880–1930 was one in which upper reaches of the corporate hierarchy were heavily infused with a deeply masculine ethic. As Rosabeth Kanter (1977) observes in her classic study, *Men and Women of the Corporation*, managers and professionals typically legitimated their growing authority and prestige by emphasizing cultural themes that were widely defined as men's traits – the ability to engage in abstract reasoning, to make decisions on the basis of rational calculation and impersonal considerations (traits that women were believed to lack). These themes were made explicit in classified advertising, which up until the 1970s listed notices in segregated "help wanted – male" and "– female" sections of the local newspapers. The combined effect of these historical and institutional processes acted to inscribe within our occupational structure a deep and abiding pattern of occupational sex-typing and gender segregation in which manual and managerial work was gendered "male," and routine office and care-giving work was gendered "female." This is why so many readers continue to be stumped by the paradox with which this chapter began.

Once established, this pattern of highly gendered work

has proven extremely difficult to uproot. Indeed, despite the surge in women's labor-force participation, the convergence of men's and women's educational and professional qualifications, and legislation that has banned the most overt forms of employment discrimination, men and women continue to be employed in starkly different domains.

Social scientists commonly use a statistical method to measure the degree of occupational segregation by sex (and race). Called the index of dissimilarity (or D), this measure tracks the proportion of workers who would need to change their occupations if an equal gender representation were to be achieved. The measure varies from a theoretical limit of 1 (a condition that might be called occupational apartheid) to 0 (a perfectly integrated occupational structure). What is most remarkable about the resulting measure is how little change occurred during the course of the last century. Three general periods can be identified. The first is the period between 1900 and 1970, when the index of dissimilarity remained almost unchanged. Then, D stood at roughly 0.70. The second is the period that began in the early 1970s, owing to the cumulative effects of the women's movement and equal employment legislation. Here, D began to fall, reaching 0.55 in 1990 – a decline of roughly a fifth. The third period is the most recent one, since 1990. Now, D has shown almost no tendency to decline (and, indeed, in recent years there have been tendencies for gender segregation to increase). Overall, this pattern indicates that the bulk of the decline in occupational segregation has been limited to the late 1970s and 1980s, and that only a glacial pace of change has occurred since that time (Cotter et al. 2004).

Nor is the pattern one of simply separate patterns of employment. Much as was true under the system of Jim Crow race relations, "separate" has implied "unequal" conditions in several respects. Thus women now account for nearly half of all graduates with medical, law, and MBA degrees (49, 47, and 44 percent, respectively, in 2007). Yet, even with these degrees in hand, women are paid significantly less. Women who do become chief executives earn roughly three-quarters (74.5 percent) of the salaries enjoyed by their male counterparts. Women in law earn almost the same proportion (74.9 percent). And women who become physicians earn only 64.2 percent of what men receive. The sources of such differences are of course complex, yet they often persist even within given professional specialties and when functional qualifications are taken into account. Moreover, women are less likely to wield supervisory and managerial authority, and more likely to oversee a predominantly female workforce when they do. Women who gain positions of authority also receive less of a pay advantage than do men. And at the upper reaches of the corporate realm, women remain outsiders. Thus, in 2010, only 12 of the Fortune 500 corporations were led by female CEOs (Reskin and Ross 1992; Reskin and Padavic 2003). When women own their own small businesses, they are more likely to operate on the margins of the business world; on average, woman-owned small businesses earn revenues that are 40 percent lower than those received by men. Finally, women remain more heavily concentrated in a handful of jobs, indicating a more constrained set of occupational opportunities than men typically experience. While the 10 largest male occupations account for roughly a fifth of all men in the paid labor force, the equivalent proportion for women is half again as large (a fact that has been constant for decades, suggesting that women have tended to be concentrated in a narrower band of sex-typed occupations).

How can this pattern of persistent occupational segregation and inequality be explained? The following discussion briefly reviews four of the most influential efforts to make sense of the gender inequality at work, commenting on the degree to which empirical findings have lent support to each approach. Each of these approaches acknowledges that overt discrimination exists and often takes its toll on women's employment opportunities. Yet each suggests that more subtle processes also unfold at work, accounting for gender disparities in ways that often escape the understanding of those who are involved.

Human Capital Theory and Supply-side Approaches

One abiding approach toward gender inequalities at work has focused especially on earnings inequality. The approach discussed here – that of human capital theory – has been advanced by economists (Becker 1964), who have focused on the production-related assets that individual workers attain. Put simply, human capital theorists view variations in earnings as reflecting differences in the productivity-related assets that workers bring with them into their jobs. In a sense, human capital theory is well named, since it treats workers' productive capacities as investments, much like the ones employers make in machines and equipment. From this perspective, the more workers invest in their own productive powers – for example, by undertaking education and training, acquiring labor-market experience, or remaining in a given job without interruption – the greater their rates of return are likely to be. In a sense, then, human capital theory views earnings disparities as reflecting the implicit choices that workers make with respect to their jobs. If women earn substantially less than do men, for example, human capital theorists predict that the reasons will stem from women's greater commitment to family life than to work (which limits their investment in education and training), or from their tendency to interrupt their careers (thus reducing their labor-market experience and tenure in a given job). If women earn lower wages and other job rewards, the reasons are expected to lie in their more modest stock of marketable assets, and lower commitment to the sphere of production as such.

Reflecting its emphasis on the worker's individual attributes and choices, human capital theorists make little effort to explain why women might be more invested in family life than in paid employment, or why they might come to hold lower occupational aspirations than do men. The latter themes are addressed by theorists who emphasize gender-role socialization. The notion here is largely congruent with human capital theory, but with a greater emphasis on the social and cultural influences that shape men's and women's values. Put simply, this approach argues that family, schooling, peer groups, and media all differentially socialize men and women, instilling distinct sets of normative orientations in each gender. Once internalized, these values are predicted to shape the attitudes and behaviors that men and women exhibit with respect to work and family. Women will forgo jobs that interfere with family life, or, more generally, that seem to contradict culturally established conceptions of femininity.

There are minor differences between these two approaches. Human-capital theory places far more emphasis on individual assets and attributes, while gender-role theory is more like to stress the importance of normative conventions and values that transcend the individual. Yet both approaches stress influences rooted in the characteristics of the workers themselves, rather than in the work organizations that employ them. In this respect, they emphasize supply-side determinants of earnings and employment, while remaining silent on the demand side of the equation (matters addressed by other theoretical approaches).

Human-capital theory seems plausible on the surface. Clearly, workers do suffer wage penalties when they withdraw from the labor market, or otherwise interrupt the continuity of their labor-force participation. And, clearly, women workers do face challenges that men do not (especially in a society that makes few provisions for paid family leave). Moreover, levels of education and training have an important impact on occupational attainment and career earnings. And women do on average exhibit fewer years of paid employment during the course of their careers. It is therefore plausible that women will suffer lower earnings than do men, especially at the later stages of their careers (when career interruptions take their toll). Yet, although it seems clear that human-capital theory has at least some validity, studies have drawn attention to abiding limitations in this explanatory approach. First, educational levels among men and women have largely converged in recent years, and women have often surpassed men with respect to high school, college, and even graduate degrees. Yet earnings inequality has not shown any secular decline, as we have seen. Second, there is no evidence that women exhibit lower levels of occupational commitment than do men. Indeed, some studies find that women tend to work harder than men in the same occupation (for reasons that can be much debated). Third, human-capital theory offers no means of explaining the persistence of wage inequalities among workers in the same occupation, with similar family situations and levels of occupational commitments. Perhaps most important of all is the fact that human-capital theory is so heavily fixated on individual-level attributes that it largely neglects the role of structural (organizational and institutional) influences that act to limit workers' access to valued job rewards (and which can thus discourage women from seeking the marketable assets needed to pursue them). As is discussed immediately below, pay levels, promotion opportunities, and the value assigned to particular types of work are all subject to social and political processes that far transcend individual-level attributes and investments.

Gender-role theory avoids some of these problems by emphasizing the culturally shaped norms, values, and identities that workers exhibit, which impact their occupational pursuits. The difficulty with gender-role theory is that it emphasizes the enduring effects of early socialization throughout the course of one's working life. Put differently, it expects gender-role socialization to shape workers' inclinations for decades, quite irrespective of the opportunities that unfold in later life. Yet, clearly, the choices workers make often seem highly malleable, and subject to variation in accordance with the opportunities that become available at any given time. Think, for example, of women workers' responses to the opening up of factory employment during the wartime mobilization at the beginning of the 1940s. Women of this generation may have been socialized in accordance with gender-appropriate behavior, but such cultural influences proved irrelevant when high-paying jobs quickly became available. The point is that cultural influences are only one among many factors that impinge on worker behavior. Indeed, they often pale in significance when work-based opportunities make themselves available.

Structural Approaches: The Demand Side of the Equation

Often developed in opposition to human-capital approaches, a number of competing models have developed that stand at odds with this approach. One important difference is that theories in this latter camp attach much more significance to the social and organizational features of the workplace itself, rather than to the attributes of individual workers. (This is why the term "structural" is sometimes used to describe such thinking.) A further difference is that theorists in this second group emphasize the *demand* side of the equation (that is, the decisions and preferences of the employers, rather than those of the workers as such). This difference is important not only for social scientific research (which orients empirical analysis in very different directions), but also for reasons involving legal culpability. By focusing on the demand size of the equation, social scientists begin to address questions that involve employer discrimination and equal employment opportunity laws (matters discussed at the end of this chapter).

One of the most influential studies in the structural vein has surely been *Men and Women of the Corporation* (1977), the above-mentioned study by the Harvard organizational studies scholar Rosabeth Moss Kanter. Breaking with human-capital theory, Kanter claimed to identify several sources of gender inequality within the social organization of the workplace itself. An in-depth analysis of workplace dynamics at a large corporate headquarters, this study made several enduring contributions to the field.

First, she emphasized the role played by homophily (or same-group preference) in the distribution of job rewards. Since managers and executives confront high levels of uncertainty in their jobs, Kanter suggests that they understandably place a premium on trust. Executives will often favor managers who share their basic assumptions about the world, in other words, and who can conform to the executive's thinking without having to be told what to do. The predictable result is that managers will exhibit a powerful tendency toward in-group selection – that is, they will select employees who closely resemble their own backgrounds and orientations about the world. The result strongly perpetuates the privileges of established elites. This emphasis on homophily has given rise to much empirical research, especially focused on the search methods that employers tend to use.

Next, and even more important, is a second line of analysis that Kanter opened up, focusing on what she termed "relative proportions." While the *absolute* size of the firm had long been a major source of concern among researchers, few researchers had studied *relative* size – that is, the effects that flow from the social or demographic composition of the group or department itself. Where women workers accounted for only a small proportion of the groups and departments within a given workplace (as in "skewed" groups), they were likely to experience three perceptual tendencies: greater visibility (and thus more intense performance pressures), an exaggeration of their differences from the dominant group (leading to heightened boundaries), and an imposition of stereotypical images or perceptions on women (even when such images were a poor fit). The sheer passage of time could not suffice to dispel the dynamics of tokenism, Kanter insisted; instead, vicious cycles of disadvantage were likely to result, only perpetuating women's subordinate positions within the firm. In this view, the structure of the organization (its generation of skewed groups) shaped the patterns of interaction that arose at work, in turn generating cycles of disadvantage that made it harder for women (and minorities) to achieve success within the firm.

Kanter's theory was especially useful for its emphasis on the relation between organizational structure and forms of workplace interaction. It has generated a broad array of studies focused on the relation between relative proportions and the perceptual tendencies she observed. Much of the research has confirmed Kanter's thinking, while also indicating the need for important modifications. For example, Blair-Loy's study of women finance executives (2001) observed a pattern of inter-group boundaries that closely conformed to Kanter's original research. Women in finance had to adopt survival strategies – for example, emphasizing their sexuality, becoming merely "one of the boys," or donning a neutered gender identity – much as Kanter had found. Yet the women in Blair-Loy's study increasingly found it possible to *vary* their survival strategies, or to combine different conceptions of gender, thus suggesting that women had gained a greater degree of flexibility than when Kanter conducted her research.

A second point of modification in Kanter's thinking has stemmed from her effort to establish a general theory of organizational exclusion – that is, a theory that could encompass not only the experience of men and women, but also those based on race, nationality, and other significant social types. Kanter's approach implied that when men were employed in skewed groups, they too would encounter social processes akin to the dynamics of tokenism. This logic suggests that the structure of the group situation would have invariant effects in female- and male-dominated settings. Either way, the numerically dominant group would use its power and centrality in ways that would peripheralize members of the out-group, multiplying the obstacles its members confront. These assumptions were directly challenged by the University of Texas sociologist Christine Williams (1992, 1995), who studied men in four occupations that are non-traditional for their sex: nursing, elementary-school teaching, librarianship, and social work. Contrary to Kanter's thinking, men in these female-dominated occupations actually experienced decided *advantages* that *facilitated* their organizational mobility, moving them upward into administrative or managerial positions much more quickly than most women found possible (an effect she called the "glass escalator"). This pattern derived from women's assumptions about men's inherent abilities, from men's ability to benefit from interaction with powerful allies in positions of power, and from expectations rooted in the wider society, the effect of which was that "despite their intentions . . . [men] face invisible pressures to move up in their professions. Like being on a moving escalator, they have to work to stay in place" (Williams 1995: 87).

Subsequent research has qualified Williams's arguments in important respects. Conducting a national study of the US nursing profession, Snyder and Green (2008) found that gender-based inequalities in this historically female occupation are complex. Gender was salient in one important respect, in that it tends to segregate male and female nurses horizontally into distinct (and unequally rewarded) specialties. Yet men did not experience any glass-escalator effect, and, indeed, did not enjoy easier movement into administrative positions. Other studies have suggested that the "escalator" effect may implicitly draw upon not only gender but also racial privilege. In her study of African-American men employed as nurses, Wingfield (2009) found that racial boundaries prevented black male nurses from establishing the advantageous relations with supervisors and patients that their white male counterparts were able to do. These studies have called for caution in extending Kanter's theory beyond male-dominated settings, and for greater attention to the intersection of race and gender in the distribution of employment opportunities.

Kanter's structural orientation is at least partly responsible for the spread of the architectural metaphors that have influenced subsequent research, in addition to the "glass escalator" notion. Even more influential has been prior research on the "glass ceiling" – a notion that gained currency within journalistic discourse (Hymowitz and Schellhardt 1986) and resulted in the 1991 establishment of a Federal Glass Ceiling Commission (see 1995a, b). The argument here is that "the disadvantages women face relative to men intensify as they move up organizational hierarchies" (Baxter and Wright 2000: 276; emphasis added). In a sense, the notion here is that not only numbers but also power within the organization matter greatly. As women ascend the corporate hierarchy, they encounter increasing levels of resistance to their encroachment on elite terrain.

Results are as yet somewhat mixed. There can be no question that women remain remarkably under-represented at the upper reaches of the corporate and professional worlds; this despite their dramatically increased numbers within law, medical, and business schools. Moreover, using the Panel Study of Income Dynamics, Union College sociologist David Cotter and his colleagues (2001) do find evidence of a glass ceiling among white and black women (but not black men): obstacles to women's attainment of highly rewarding jobs·do seem to increase as they ascend the economic ladder. Findings reported by David Maume (2004) largely replicate this pattern, here finding a gulf between opportunities for white men and for other gender and racial groups. Still, the findings on the glass ceiling are somewhat mixed and require more research before firm conclusions can be drawn. For one thing, Rosalind Baxter and Erik Olin Wright (2000) found no evidence of an intensified disadvantage within the United States, and only limited support for the same hypothesis in Sweden and Australia. Elizabeth Gorman and Julie Kmec (2009) studied the chances of women attorneys to achieve partner status (a much-sought and highly rewarding position). They found that women have equal probability of being hired for entry-level positions within law firms, but that as they seek to rise into positions as full partners, they suffer sharply reduced opportunities relative to men (much as glass-ceiling models predict). Interestingly, only when women have *already been made* partner are they able to compete on an equal basis with men. This pattern suggests that to succeed in the law, women must have their abilities "certified" by an external organization, and only then can compete on something resembling a level playing field. The Gorman and Kmec study is important, in that it demonstrates the need to disentangle the complex labor markets in which men and women compete for highly valued positions.

Social Networks: The Web of Affiliations

One suggestive line of analysis that may well begin to account for gender disparities at the upper reaches of work organizations centers on the social networks in which people are embedded, both at work and in the wider society. This approach begins with the premise that information about job openings is not randomly distributed among job seekers, but is in fact highly patterned in ways that can perpetuate gender (and racial) inequalities. In some formulations, the information, influence, and prestige that job seekers enjoy is a function of the stock of social resources on which they can draw. These resources are sometimes conceived as "social capital," a resource that has been defined as "the ability of actors to secure benefits by virtue of membership in social networks or other social structures" (Portes 1998). The question is whether women's social and occupational positions deprive them of the types and amounts of social capital that men enjoy, in turn reinforcing gender disparities in the distribution of employment opportunity.

Studies of social networks and gender inequality have increasingly answered this question in the affirmative (see McDonald and Day 2010; Huffman and Torres 2002). Several points have emerged in this literature. First, a substantial number of job openings are filled on the basis of informal referrals, rather than formal job announcements and formal or public recruitment strategies. This indicates that social networks hold substantial importance in accounting for disparities in access to employment opportunities. Second, the flow of job leads tends to be highly gendered, with women learning about job openings from other women, and men from other men. Third, the social networks of women and minorities tend to include fewer linkages to powerful and high-status actors than do the networks of white men. Fourth, reflecting the greater family obligations traditionally imposed on women, their social networks generally include a greater proportion of kin-based ties than do men's social networks (which tend to be more employment-based).

These differences do indeed have significant consequences for the distribution of employment opportunity: networks with a higher proportion of white males generate not only more job leads, but also job leads of higher quality (entailing access to higher-paying jobs) than do networks with higher compositions of women or minorities. In their study of a large California job-searching program, for example, Huffman and Torres (2002) found that the higher the female composition of one's network, the poorer the quality of the job leads one is likely to hear. Women who have at least some men in their networks are significantly less likely to be employed in sex-typed jobs even when other variables are held constant. Interestingly, in their recent national study of social-network ties and employment information, McDonald, Lin, and Ao (2009) found that the gender composition of one's social network becomes increasingly significant as one rises in the organizational hierarchy (just as literature on the glass ceiling predicts). Finally, McDonald and Day (2010) found that social networks have important effects even among employees who are not searching for new jobs. Spontaneously shared information about employment opportunities seems to favor white male employees, whose networks better position them to hear about job openings and to benefit from informal patterns of recruitment.

Much more remains to be known about how social networks operate, and the extent to which they account for gender disparities in access to workplace authority and career opportunities generally. From one perspective, since much social capital is formed outside the boundaries of formal organizations, and takes shape in ways that are beyond the control of any given group, it represents an effect that is beyond the reach of anti-discrimination efforts. This, however, is an overly narrow view. For one thing, research on social networks and social capital has repeatedly pointed to the inequality-producing effects that flow from firm-level recruitment strategies. Put simply, when companies rely on personal contacts and informal job referrals to fill job vacancies, the results tend to reproduce already-established patterns of gender and racial exclusion. The implication is that social movements and public policy ought to press firms to refrain from using such job recruitment methods, and stress more public or formal channels of information dissemination and referral.

A further point concerns managerial efforts (such as mentoring programs) to shape the patterns of affiliation that develop within firm boundaries. Just as organizations have become aware of the importance of workplace culture as it impinges on performance and employee behavior, so too have managers become aware of the importance of networks, at times seeking to lead the patterns of affiliation within the firm in more equitable directions via mentoring programs and programs seeking to broaden the webs of affiliation in which employees are embedded. The empirical literature on mentoring suggests that such programs do at times enhance the social ties and job-related information that female employees enjoy. Interestingly, however, same-sex mentoring programs (in which senior women are asked to coach or advocate for junior women) seem to have limited effects, perhaps because they tend to reproduce the very sex-segregated networks that limit women's opportunities. Likewise, cross-race mentoring efforts often fail, much as literature on homophily would predict. In their influential study of diversity practices, Kalev, Dobbin, and Kelley (2006) found that the adoption of mentoring programs did increase the odds of black women's entry into management positions. It remains to be seen whether social networking programs (for example, the increasingly popular LinkedIn) affect the gender composition of social networks, impacting the flow of job leads and employment outcomes more generally.

The Devaluation of Women's Work

Kanter was one of the first social scientists to emphasize the impact of relative numbers on the distribution of opportunity within the firm. In recent years, social scientists have explored the impact of relative proportions, though in ways that depart from her approach in two distinct ways.

First, the analysis here is couched not at the level of the group or department (as in Kanter's analysis), but rather at the level of the firm or the occupation. And, second, the emphasis in this developing approach is less on women's exclusion from highly rewarding jobs than on the perceptions and rewards that employers bring to bear on the jobs where work is concentrated. The argument here, which draws inspiration from the "comparable worth" movement of the 1980s, is a straightforward one. When an occupation comes to be dominated numerically by women, then managers begin to view its value through a biased lens. Put simply, the more feminized an occupation's workforce, the lower the status and pay its incumbents will enjoy, even when the objective demands of the job are held constant.

As the link between gender composition and job rewards has been debated, two general lines of analysis have been advanced. In one view, the erosion of job rewards *precedes* feminization. The notion here is that occupations undergoing de-skilling find it increasingly difficult to recruit employees with alternative routes to mobility; hence men tend to exit, and employers are compelled to rely on female labor to fill positions that more privileged males refuse (Reskin and Roos 1990). An alternative formulation is one in which the erosion of job rewards *follows* from the feminization of the occupation's incumbents. Put differently, the notion is that "work in predominantly female jobs will be devalued by both employers and prospective employees" and that "pay in predominantly female jobs is lower *because* women fill the jobs" (Levanon, England, and Allison 2009: 868). The bulk of the literature has lent support to the latter explanatory approach, providing a relatively strong and growing body of evidence suggesting that the feminization of work does indeed tend to erode incumbents' job rewards.

One early example of such research is that of the University of Massachusetts sociologist Tomaskovic-Devey (1993), who used a statewide study of workers and jobs in North Carolina to unpack the sources of earnings inequality by both gender and race. The results were complex, in that different dynamics seemed to drive pay disparities along gender and racial lines. Interestingly, the findings provided strong support for the devaluation thesis. After taking into account the human capital of workers, the skill requirements of their jobs, and the industries in which they were employed, a clear trend emerged in which the gender composition of an occupation had significant and negative effects on the pay of the women and men performing the job. Comparable effects did not exist for race.

Two limitations of this study – its cross-sectional nature and relatively small sample size – have since been overcome by numerous studies. Most notable is the work of the Stanford sociologist Paula England and her colleagues (England, Allison, and Wu 2007; Levanon, England, and Allison 2009). Using detailed census data to capture trends over multiple decades, these scholars find a repeated pattern in which highly feminized occupations suffer wage deterioration over time, with little or no evidence of a reverse effect. Using a slightly different approach and source of data, Catanzarite (2003) tracked the impact on white men's wages as the demography of an occupation changed during the two decades after 1971. The results again suggested that wages erode as women enter an occupation in significant numbers, even after job demands are taken into account. Finally, Cohen and Huffman (2003) extended this line of research, reporting that the devaluation of women's work is especially strong in metropolitan areas that are themselves highly sex-segregated.

This line of analysis is not only well established and highly suggestive, but has obvious implications for our understanding of discrimination too. It also directs attention to the processes that inform wage determination and job evaluation. Yet important issues remain unresolved on this terrain. One question is whether the gender and racial composition of occupations have similar effects. Do sex-typing and race-typing operate in precisely the same way? More research is needed to resolve this question, but it would seem reasonable to acknowledge salient disparities in the working out of gender and racial inequalities. Racial segregation is deeply built into the spatial landscape, thus affecting access to neighborhoods and schools in ways that have no analogue with respect to gender segregation. Hence the mechanisms that exclude women and minorities may bear a family resemblance, but are likely to operate in significantly different ways, and our theoretical frameworks should acknowledge this point.

A further source of uncertainty here concerns the precise mechanisms that account for the devaluation of the work done by women and minorities (Reskin 2003). The great bulk of commentary in this genre of research assumes that the erosion of job rewards that follows from the feminization of a given occupation is rooted in cultural biases. Women's skills and production knowledge are assigned a lower value, in other words, owing to the lesser status or prestige that women's work enjoys. Yet, clearly, *other* mechanisms may be at work quite apart from (or in league with) such cultural or normative biases. Most important perhaps is the lesser economic or labor-market *power* that women can wield when they encounter rigid constraints on their social and economic mobility. This point begins to emerge in the above-mentioned studies by Cohen and Huffman and by Catanzarite, both of which emphasize the labor-market vulnerability that women suffer in highly segregated labor-market settings. Such vulnerability (and not merely cultural biases) may allow men to exact the full value of their labor (or more), while implicitly denying women the organizational resources that are needed to do likewise. This is an important distinction to make, since different remedies will flow from these two separate approaches toward labor-market inequalities.

A final point concerning the devaluation of women's work relates to the contrast between this approach and the human-capital theory outlined above. Human-capital theory has proved enormously influential within courts charged with ruling on cases alleging gender discrimination in pay. Save for cases in which a smoking gun has emerged or where statistical inequities were indefensible, the courts have by and large viewed pay disparities between men's and women's jobs as stemming from market-based processes rooted outside the work organization, and thus as lying beyond the zone of judicial intervention.[2]

Responding to this judicial pattern, Robert L. Nelson and William Bridges (1999) have raised important questions about the empirical assumptions on which it rests. These authors selected four important cases in which courts were asked to adjudicate claims alleging pay discrimination between traditionally men's and women's jobs. Using available quantitative data on pay levels that emerged in these suits, the authors sought to determine whether market forces in fact accounted for the pay disparities that arose. Several findings emerged. First, the data indicate that the courts overlooked compelling indications that pay levels were not a function of market forces alone. In all four cases, the evidence indicated that social and organizational influences often underlay the allocation of pay raises, generating sharp inequalities over time that had no basis in the labor market. Often, pay disparities were a function of the level of organizational power wielded by department heads, or the levels of cohesion and informal alliances that were enjoyed by different groups of employees. The general conclusion Nelson and Bridges reach is that organizational politics exerts an abiding influence over pay levels in ways that courts have been slow to perceive. By embracing overly narrow interpretations of the actual drivers of gender-based pay disparities, the courts have actually helped to legitimate employer-based inequalities, rendering courts "important participants in the institutional construction of markets and the gender gap in pay" (1999: 3). Perhaps the most important finding here was that, again, pay disparities did not seem to be rooted in culturally biased evaluations of women's work, but in organizational dynamics affecting the distribution of power and efficacy within the firm as such. This argument reinforces calls for a "relational" framework of gender inequality that is attuned to the exercise of organizational power (Avent-Holt and Tomaskovic-Devey 2010). It also points to the need for greater dialogue between the legal and judicial community, on the one hand, and social science scholars studying gender disparities, on the other hand.

Conclusions

It seems hard to dispute the fact that the movements for greater gender equality have met with increasing rigidity and resistance on the part of many established institutions. Even a recent legislative victory for the pay equity movement – the Lily Ledbetter Fair Pay Act of 2009 – did no more than ensure that women have a six-month period of time during which to file claims of pay discrimination. In other words, the Ledbetter Act merely restored an administrative convention (the "pay accrual" doctrine) that had been overturned by an overly zealous, right-wing court. It is not without reason that women's organizations have spoken of a "stalled revolution." Ironically, at least some of this plateau effect may stem from the loss of momentum of the women's movement itself. As young women have enjoyed new opportunities at work, however limited they may be, the need for continued action seems less and less apparent from their point of view.

If political momentum has been lost, however, it seems clear that social science theory and research have contributed an increasingly sophisticated understanding of gender inequalities at work. The studies discussed in this chapter suggest that the perpetuation of gender segregation and disparities in access to job rewards do not stem from any single determinant. It is surely true that supply-side factors (investments in human capital) play a role in the generation of pay disparities. Yet it is also true that other, more arbitrary, factors also weigh heavily in the allocation of job rewards among women and men. Boundaries arise within work groups, often rendering women's inclusion much more difficult in corporate settings than is true for men. Patterns of interaction often trap women in roles that are not of their own choosing, or that stand at odds with their preferred attributes. The social networks, hiring practices, and patterns of affiliation and support that exist within many organizations act to reproduce the patterns of male privilege that were set in motion many decades ago. And the demographic composition of given occupations (especially the proportion of the incumbents who are female) has been shown to influence, in a complex manner, the job rewards that women can expect to enjoy.

Yet there are forces that provide grounds for confidence that further gains will prove possible, and that movement toward a truly level playing field can be made. Although many courts have adopted narrow rulings on pay equity cases, recent research by the University of Texas sociologist Sheryl Skaggs (2008) demonstrates that even the act of litigation itself has both short- and long-term effects on the proportion of managerial positions that are held by women. Other research suggests that organizations that adopt practices that visibly support gender equality (such as favorable work and family policies) derive significant benefits in the form of higher prices for their stock. Further, some evidence exists to indicate that efforts to pursue less bureaucratic "flexible" forms of work (as discussed in the preceding chapter) have the effect of disrupting long-established gender hierarchies, opening up greater opportunity for women in managerial positions (Kalev 2009). These changes are unfolding more slowly than seems fair or desirable, yet they seem certain to move forward nonetheless.

5

Ascriptive Inequalities, II: Race, Ethnicity, and Diversity at Work

The study of racial and ethnic boundaries at work has a long history in American sociology, reaching back to the work of W. E. B. Du Bois, one of the first scholars to document the injuries that racial discrimination inflicted on black workers, and to the Chicago School of sociology, whose adherents brought to light the informal patterns of exclusion that black and minority workers encountered in the years preceding the civil rights movement. Some of the more enduring contributions were made by Herbert Blumer (1958), E. C. Hughes (1994 [1951]), and Oliver Cromwell Cox (1948), all of whom sought to understand the social and cultural mechanisms that perpetuated the subordinate positions that minority workers held within the North and the South alike.

Since these scholars wrote, the struggle for racial equality at work has made remarkable gains toward equal employment opportunity. The 1964 Civil Rights Act not only barred discrimination on the basis of race and ethnicity (and gender); it also charged the Equal Employment Opportunity Commission with the task of monitoring employers' progress, and of adjudicating violations of minority workers' rights. Before the 1960s, of course, major social institutions confined black workers to the most marginal of positions. Few large corporations employed blacks in anything other than menial or dangerous jobs. Professional schools only rarely admitted black applicants. And labor organizations either excluded racial and ethnic minorities entirely, or (where this was not possible) organized separate local unions for their members. Owing to the mobilization of black Church leaders, progressive unionists, and social movement activists in both the North and the South, a sea change occurred in the 1960s and early 1970s. Armed with federal intervention, and backed by a major shift in public opinion, the civil rights movement succeeded in dismantling many of the trappings of racial and ethnic segregation at work. As court rulings were handed down in the 1970s, demonstrating an unflagging federal commitment to equal employment opportunity, the nation's largest corporations adopted an array of personnel practices that sought to symbolize the corporate commitment to racial and ethnic equality at work. To compare the entering class of elite law schools (or, for that matter, rank-and-file union leaders) before and after the peak of the civil rights movement is to encounter evidence of a dramatic shift in the opportunity structures throughout the United States.

There can be no denying that US society has taken major steps toward equal employment opportunity. The proportion of blacks who live in poverty, for example, has dramatically fallen since the middle of the twentieth century. Racial and ethnic disparities in education have been significantly reduced. Black representation in the skilled trades has increased substantially. And whereas the most common employment opportunity for black women in 1960 was that of domestic work – a legacy of the subservient positions blacks held under slavery – by 1980, the largest proportion of black women held jobs in administrative-support occupations (much as did white women). Indeed, as African Americans entered into middle-class positions, some social scientists began to lament the resulting pattern of out-migration from the nation's cities – a development that deprived poor and minority communities of the leadership and organizational capacity they previously enjoyed (Wilson 1996). Black gains have been so dramatic that many whites have come to conclude that policies in support of equal employment opportunity are no longer warranted. Attitude surveys now commonly find that respondents believe that public policy has bent the stick too far in the opposite direction, actually favoring minorities at the expense of whites.

Indeed, it is tempting to conclude that the contemporary workplace has left its troubled racial past behind. However comforting this thought may be, the evidence to the contrary – discussed immediately below – is simply undeniable. Racial and ethnic boundaries at work have persisted, though they have taken new and often more subtle forms than before. Paradoxically, efforts to achieve a "color-blind" milieu, or to celebrate diversity, may at times tend to perpetuate the very inequalities they seek to uproot. The task of much sociological research, in fact, is to shed light on the mechanisms that perpetuate racial inequality – to render visible the sources of racial inequality that might otherwise remain hidden from public view.

This chapter thus extends our analysis of ascriptive inequalities to the terrain of racial and ethnic relations at work. We ask some important questions. In what ways, and to what extent, have work organizations fallen short of the ideal of equal employment opportunity? What social and organizational mechanisms have reproduced racial and ethnic disparities? Why have employers so fervently embraced the concept of "diversity," and what is meant by this often-used concept? And what organizational practices might foster a truly inclusive workplace – one in which members of all groups can derive a sense of common cause?

The Continuing Significance of Race at Work

Despite clear equalizing trends in education and employment, official statistics indicate that there are abiding disparities in occupational attainment by race and ethnicity. Racial and ethnic minorities (blacks and Latinos) remain significantly over-represented in manual occupations, and severely under-represented in management and professional occupations. These disparities are especially pronounced among men, and are discernible even if we use broad occupational categories (which significantly underestimate occupational inequalities across groups). Thus, the Current Population Survey of 2009 reveals that the occupational distribution of white men is highly skewed toward prestigious jobs (for example, managerial and professional jobs); white men are more than twice as likely to work in such reward-ing office jobs (39.3 percent) as to perform manual work (only 15.6 percent of white men hold production, trans-portation, and material-moving jobs). By contrast, manual work holds a much more salient place in the working lives of African-American men. For the latter group, manual jobs are the single largest occupational category (with the managerial and professional levels of this category now nearing parity with manual jobs). The pattern among Latinos is similar to that of blacks, though somewhat more pro-nounced. Latinos, too, are more heavily clustered in manual occupations that carry lesser prestige.

These are terribly broad occupational categories, of course, which do not take levels of education into account. For this reason, research conducted by the economist Derrick Hamilton (2006) is of particular value. Hamilton studied 475 detailed occupational categories and took into account the availability of qualified job applicants in any given labor-market locale. What he found was a pronounced pattern of racialized occupational location. Black men tended to be significantly under-represented in the most prestigious job categories, despite the availability of eligible applicants, and to be over-represented in the least prestigious jobs. In only a minority of jobs (roughly 15 percent) were blacks represented in rough proportion to their numbers in the labor market. Other studies reinforce and extend the point, showing that minority workers tend to be concentrated in jobs that are largely held by other minority workers. For example, the Washington State sociologist Julie Kmec (2003) used data on the labor-market patterns evident in Atlanta, Boston, and Los Angeles, and reported that 44 percent of blacks hold jobs that employ a largely black workforce, while 48 percent of Latinos work in largely Latino jobs. Very few whites work in jobs that show such high levels of minority concentrations.

Moreover, experimental and survey evidence consist-ently suggests that labor markets commonly deny minority workers opportunities that white workers enjoy even when levels of skill, experience, and job-relevant factors are rigor-ously controlled. Consider first the audit studies repeatedly carried out by the Urban Institute, a Washington, DC-based social policy institution. Although these studies are subject to some debate, they are useful in sensitizing us to the presence of racial disparities in job searches by dominant and minority group members. Research in this vein typically sends matched pairs of job applicants who are trained and equipped to present potential employers with identical job skills and applications, and to engage in similar forms of interaction. Thus all job-relevant characteristics are held constant, save for the question of race. Although there are some variations, the most prevalent pattern in cities such as Washington, Chicago, New York, and other urban areas is one in which white job applicants are much more likely to receive favorable employment outcomes (that is, to be given a job application at all, to be called back for an interview, or to be offered a position) than are minorities (Favreault 2008). A parallel set of findings emerges from the experiments conducted by Bertrand and Mullainathan (2004), who sent résumés to potential employers in Boston and Chicago. The latter authors again used identical job applications, but varied the résumés only by the first name of the applicants, with some résumés using "white" first names (Emily or Greg) and others using "black" first names (for example, Lakisha or Jamal). Again, sharp disparities emerged in the results. White applicants were 50 percent more likely to receive callbacks, and employers were more attentive to the skills reported on their résumés than was the case for blacks. Finally, Pager (2003) trained white and black job applicants and allowed their backgrounds to vary not only by race but also by criminal record. Her findings indicate that white applicants who reported felony convictions were slightly more likely to receive favorable treatment from employers than were black applicants with clean records.

Further studies in this vein have used survey methods to identify the factors impinging on access to supervisory positions, while holding constant human capital variables such as education, training, and labor-market experience. The results suggest that labor markets continue to favor white employees. Maume (1999) finds that whites are twice as likely to gain access to promotion as are black and Latino workers, even when human capital and industrial sector are held constant. R. A. Smith (1997, 2001) finds that these disparities in the distribution of job authority have remained unchanged during the last two decades. Smith and Elliott (2002) find that the selection of supervisors often embodies a pattern of ethnic matching, which limits minority supervisors to positions overseeing co-ethnic employees. Research on the relationship between supervisors and subordinates finds that dominant group supervisors issue harsher job evaluations in cases involving minority workers rather than whites, again holding constant job-related qualifications (Ibarra 1995; Avey, West, and Crossley 2008).

Thus, after several decades of public policy favoring equal employment opportunity, and after large-scale mobilizations of minority communities, unequal treatment seems to constitute a pervasive feature of the American labor market. Indeed, recent studies by Tomaskovic-Devey and his colleagues (2006) indicate that the racial and ethnic desegregation in US workplaces has largely stalled in the decades since the early 1980s.

How can we account for these patterns? At least some of the explanatory frameworks that scholars have advanced run parallel to those that have been applied to gender inequality (as discussed in the previous chapter). Indeed, many studies seek to compare and disentangle the separate and combined effects of race and gender, with results that are discussed below. Yet, as mentioned, the factors that drive racial and gender disparities do not neatly align with one another in any simple manner, as patterns of segregation at work, in neighborhoods, schools, and other institutions obviously take quite different forms. Moreover, race and gender often intersect in ways that acquire highly complex and sometimes surprising forms.

In what follows, we briefly survey theory and research that bears on the persistence of racial disparities in the access to job rewards. I leave to one side the literature on human capital arguments, partly owing to space limitations, and partly to the intricate and uncertain state of our knowledge on this terrain.[1] I focus the chapter's attention on four general classes of explanatory factors that have been emphasized in the literature (some of which have been broached with respect to gender): social closure processes; social networks and hiring practices; the devaluation of minority workers' labor; and emerging concepts of diversity themselves.

Social Closure Processes

Max Weber assigned the concept of social closure a central role in his analysis of economic and social inequality ([1903] 1978). In Weber's work, social closure referred to the structural and ideological mechanisms that privileged groups invoked in an effort to minimize competition over scarce resources (cf. Parkin 1979; Tomaskovic-Devey 1993; Roscigno et al. 2007). Social closure is about "opportunity hoarding," or the monopolization of advantages by privileged groups. As such, it may be more or less explicit, more or less consciously enacted, and either legal or extra-legal, depending on the social and historical context (Light, Roscigno, and Kalev 2011; Roscigno, Garcia, and Bobbitt-Zeher 2009). It may or may not be coterminous with discrimination. Roscigno and his colleagues have used cases of anti-discriminatory litigation in the state of Ohio to show how some of the more blatant forms of social closure operate to limit the opportunities of women and minorities and to maintain racial and gender hierarchies at work. Other analysts address more subtle and legal forms of social closure, as in the case of Collins's (1979) study of credentialism and labor-market exclusion, Moss and Tilly's (1996) study of "soft skills" and racial exclusion, or McIlwee and Robinson's (1992) analysis of the ways in which the masculinist culture of engineering limits the careers of female engineers. Increasingly, researchers have acknowledged the importance of the cultural practices and symbolic representations that unfold at work, and that can exert a significant influence on the employment prospects of workers in virtually any occupational context (Vallas 2001). Key to this strand of thinking is the argument that the mechanisms used to exclude potential rivals are highly arbitrary constructs that privileged groups use when seeking to limit the competition they face from would-be competitors. To use terms introduced by Robert Merton, such patterns of inequality portray non-functional characteristics as prerequisites of the job (cited in Reskin and Padavic 2003: 37).

The importance of social closure for an understanding of racial and ethnic disparities is underscored in the above-mentioned study of North Carolina workers (Tomaskovic-Devey 1993), which found that the lower pay received by black workers in North Carolina was primarily due to their exclusion from skilled, higher-paying jobs, even after levels of human capital had been taken into account. In the view of some theorists, the intensity of social-closure efforts is predicted to rise in direct proportion to the size of the minority group, for dominant group members perceive a growing threat to their privileges as their rivals grow in size and potential strength (see Blalock 1967; cf. Blumer 1958). And, indeed, a number of studies do find that the job evaluations, promotion chances, and/or pay levels that minority workers receive all tend to suffer where minority workers constitute a larger proportion of the group, department, or firm. The greater the relative size of the minority group, the greater the threat its members seem to pose, and the harsher the response job incumbents provide (Baldi and McBrier 1997; Braddock and McPartland 1987; Maume 1999; Tienda and Lii 1987; Tomaskovic-Devey 1993).

Social closure can at times be linked to the spatial distribution of workers within the workplace itself. The ecology of the work setting is often bound up with the racial or ethnic status of the worker; many factories, hospitals, restaurants, and hotels still position minority workers within back offices, kitchen areas, or service and cleaning spaces far removed from public contact or visibility. As in residential communities, spatial segregation within the workplace powerfully constrains the movements and activities of minority employees, which, in turn, affects their opportunities for interaction with dominant-group workers, limits their access to production skills and job information, and hinders their chances of establishing informal ties to dominant-group employees. The spatial location of minority workers may also symbolize or reaffirm their marginal position within the firm. In a study of traditional manufacturing settings in the American South, I found that black workers were often assigned to production areas in the basement or lowest levels of factory buildings, symbolizing their place within the racial hierarchy at work (Vallas 2003b). Workplace terrain can carry racial significance by providing tacit markers of the places which members of dominant and minority groups are expected to hold within the work organization, fueling conflict when such boundaries are transgressed (Blumer 1958; Lee 2000).

One of the more illuminating lines of analysis that has opened up in recent years can be found in Roscigno's use of longitudinal data drawn from anti-discrimination lawsuits filed in the state of Ohio (Roscigno, Garcia, and Bobbitt-Zeher 2007; Roscigno, Hodson, and Lopez 2009; Light, Roscigno, and Kalev 2011). These data provide a rich and illustrative source of evidence on the discriminatory treatment many workers suffer, and the perceptions and rationalizations that employers bring to bear on such practices. Yet, while such data sensitize us to the harsh and inhospitable treatment many workers encounter, the use of the legal or judicial system as the source of data collection limits the resulting view to actionable cases, rather than the more subtle, unconscious patterns of behavior that probably account for the unequal treatment faced by members of subordinate groups.

Social Networks and Hiring Practices

Implied throughout the foregoing chapters is a truism that bears repeating: workers do not enter into firms as atomized entities. Nor are jobs commonly filled through purely formal advertising and selection processes. Rather, job-related information and job referrals flow along the conduits of social networks. Thus embeddedness in networks that link job seekers to employers can be a decisive factor affecting employment outcomes. Moreover, such networks are greatly influenced by culturally rooted preferences, residential location, and community-based patterns of affiliation. Given the deeply segregated nature of so much of American social life, it seems likely that the webs of affiliation in which job seekers are embedded will have an important impact on their employment outcomes.

In fact, there is a large and growing body of findings that provides support for this point of view. One example is the case study by the New York University sociologist Deirdre Royster (2003), who explored the labor-market experiences of a group of working-class students undergoing vocational training at a high school near Baltimore, Maryland. The white and black students in her study all had similar levels of performance in school and similar levels of motivation.

All did roughly equivalent work in their classes, and were keen to establish themselves in their vocations. Yet the black students encountered a much rockier road to career success than did the white students, not because of overt discrimination or racial preferences, but because of a subtler and less pernicious fact: the white students were more strongly embedded in social networks that linked them to job opportunities and to prospective employers. They had an easier time establishing relationships with their teachers, enjoying a greater level of sponsorship. But, more than this, they enjoyed ties to employers (many of whom were alumni of their own high school) that black students did not possess. Despite such labor market advantages, white students often believed the deck had been stacked *against* them, and that they had succeeded in spite of social biases favoring *blacks*. The upshot of Royster's study was that the structures of social relations in which job seekers exist can have powerful effects on the employment outcomes that unfold across racial and ethnic lines.

Are these findings generalizable? Although there is some uncertainty as to precisely how hiring networks operate, the answer is clearly yes. For example, Berkeley sociologist Trond Petersen and his colleagues (Petersen, Saporta, and Seidel 2000) amassed data from 10 years' worth of job applications at a medium-sized high-technology company, using these data to identify factors affecting employment outcomes. The processes handling job applications of men and women seemed largely meritocratic, once age and education were controlled, and little network effect seemed to occur. In the case of race, however, employment outcomes were strongly influenced by the network connections that applicants enjoyed. For one thing, the greatest proportion of the minority applicants (blacks, Latinos, and Native Americans) applied through formal channels (job announcements, university referrals), while whites were far more likely to utilize informal friendship networks as their means of entry into the firm. Moreover, once the network connection was statistically controlled, all racial and ethnic differences in employment outcomes disappeared.

The importance of network ties also emerged in research conducted by Kasinitz and Rosenberg, who studied the labor-market experiences of poor black residents in Red Hook (near the Brooklyn waterfront). Although they lived directly near high-wage manual jobs at the docks, black residents lacked the social connections and referral ties needed to gain access to these jobs. More than spatial contiguity or motivation was needed to gain admission to this domain; what was needed was the ability to wield social network ties.

Again, it is tempting to view social network influences as lying beyond the control of the employer. These influences seem to stem from the interpersonal webs of affiliation that arise in social life, thus involving patterns of homophily that are not necessarily job-induced. Yet this conclusion is highly misleading. Social networks operate not only off the job but on it as well. Patterns of interaction at work, forms of sponsorship, and mentoring all operate to help or hinder the transmission of job-relevant information, skills, and production expertise. It thus behooves employers to take note of these facts, and to cultivate forms of affiliation that are in fact conducive to equal employment opportunity. The study by Kalev, Dobbin, and Kelly (2006), discussed further below, indicates that formal mentoring programs and other practices that aim to embed minority and women workers within workplace networks have begun to latch on, with beneficial effects.

Even more important is the fact that employers often rely on informal networks as a mode of employee selection. Doing so can provide a cheap and effective means of recruiting reliable employees. But using informal networks and referrals to fill rewarding jobs can over time have real consequences for equal opportunity, since doing so tends to perpetuate existing patterns of racial and ethnic inequality. Typical here are the findings reported by the University of North Carolina demographer Ted Mouw (2002), who finds that the method of employee referral is at least as significant a determinant of occupational segregation as is geographic proximity (a factor that has received substantial discussion in the literature). Relying on employee referral to fill blue-collar jobs increases occupational segregation by roughly 10 percent (effects that are then compounded over time).

Race-Typing and the Devaluation of Black Labor

The race-typing of certain occupations is a long-standing phenomenon in many cultures. Its logic is one that compels members of marginalized groups to perform tasks that more privileged groups view as abhorrent or unclean. Though these tasks vary, depending on what is deemed sacred and what profane, "dirty" work often includes the handling of the dead, the skinning of animals, or dealings with human waste. In some societies, such work carries an intensely symbolic value, in that it publicly symbolizes the inferiority of those compelled to perform it – and, by implication, it reaffirms the superiority of those who benefit from such work.

Western societies are not immune to this phenomenon. Especially during the Jim Crow era, black men were often compelled to work in servile jobs as handymen or as railroad porters, and black women as maids. Echoes of this phenomenon can perhaps be found in the concentration of immigrant Latino workers in food-processing or landscape-maintenance work, and in the ethnic division of labor that exists in many restaurants and hotels. As work has grown increasingly formalized, however, and as professional approaches toward human resource management have grown more salient, the most obvious linkages between dirty work and dark skin may well have faded into the past.

But the question arises as to whether the race-typing of work may still influence the value that employers attach to the minority workers' jobs, if in more furtive ways. Does the minority composition of a job affect the pay its incumbents receive, even after taking into account such factors as skill requirements, industry, establishment size, and economic sector? This question has attracted a fair amount of research, some of which has produced mixed results (cf. Tomaskovic-Devey 1993 and Catanzarite 2003). On balance, however, the evidence seems to indicate that the racial composition of given occupations does indeed reach into the value attached to workers' jobs, devaluing certain types of work because of the demographic composition of the job. Again, as with gender, the specific mechanisms that underlie this effect remain to be unearthed.

This link between race-typing and devaluation is reported in the study by Julie Kmec that was briefly mentioned above. Kmec used data from the Multi-City Study of Urban Inequality, focusing on the labor-market situation of 635 workers employed in Atlanta, Boston, and Los Angeles. The question she addressed was whether the occupational segregation of minority workers undermines the pay that workers receive. The study is especially notable for its ability to disentangle the effects of demographic concentration at multiple levels of analysis (the job, the occupation, and the establishment), while controlling for rival factors that can affect wage levels (such as establishment size, industry, and levels of human capital). Kmec's findings are instructive in several respects. First, employment in minority-dominated contexts does indeed depress the wages of minority (and white) workers, after adjusting for other influences. Second, this wage penalty operates mainly at the level of the job, rather than the occupation or establishment. Third, and perhaps most important, is the magnitude of the wage penalty that minority workers typically face: a reduction in hourly wages of 18 percent in the case of workers employed at largely black jobs, and 15 percent for workers in jobs that are largely held by Latinos. As Kmec observes (2003: 52), this means that "the monetary loss associated with working in a full-time, year-round job with mostly Latino workers totals nearly $3,500 and over $4,200 for those in mostly black jobs."

Because Kmec studied workers at a single point in time, she could not rule out the possibility that wages eroded first, and that occupational segregation by race was an *effect* of the lower pay she observed rather than a *cause*. Given this uncertainty, the study by Washington State sociologist Lisa Catanzarite (2003) is especially helpful. This author used longitudinal survey data to trace the effects of demographic composition during two periods of time: 1971–81 and 1982–92. She found that occupational composition does indeed affect pay levels, rather than the reverse causal ordering. Equally important, she argues that wage disparities were not rooted only in cultural biases (a "status contamination" effect), but largely reflected differences in the labor-market power, collective capacity, and bargaining efficacy of the different racial and ethnic groups. Here again, as with research on gender, more research is needed on the precise mechanisms that underlie the wage penalties that flow from occupational segregation by race and ethnicity.

The Concept of Diversity: Reinforcing Inequality?

One of the most important developments in managerial thinking about equal employment opportunity has been the increasing prevalence of business rhetoric that uses the concept of diversity as its touchstone. Actually, the term "uses" might be an understatement; the term "celebrates" perhaps better captures the meanings that managers have attached to the phenomenon. It is fair to say that business journalists, magazines, and managerial periodicals have all trumpeted the concept of diversity, viewing it as a means of enriching the performance potential of work groups, departments, and whole firms. Where this support for the diversity construct is approached systematically (as in research conducted by industrial and organizational psychologists), it typically argues that groups whose members bring heterogeneous sets of experiences to the firm are likely to make better decisions as a result. Differing perspectives will, in other words, deepen the process of deliberation and enable groups to avoid narrow, parochial, or outmoded assumptions (Ancona and Caldwell 1992; Williams and O'Reilly 1998). So enthused is the reception that business audiences have provided for the diversity construct that human resource managers have broadened the meaning of diversity in multiple ways. Rather than simply applying to demographic or ascribed statuses (gender, race, ethnicity, age, or nationality), it has increasingly expanded to include lifestyle, educational background, appearance, and other sources of cultural difference. Understandably, perhaps, a justly famous episode of the television show *The Office* subjects this corporate orientation to withering critique.

There are several reasons why a critical assessment of the diversity construct would seem to be in order. First, as shown in the research of Lauren Edelman, now a dean at the University of California Berkeley law school, the concept of diversity has gained currency by dislodging older, civil rights conceptions that grew out of the legislative, judicial, and executive branch interventions of the 1960s and 1970s (Edelman, Fuller, and Mara-Drita 2001). Studying the rhetoric employed in managerial journals and other publications during the last quarter of the twentieth century, Edelman finds that the popularity of the diversity construct expanded prodigiously at precisely the moment when the language of equal employment opportunity and affirmative action was disappearing from the managerial lexicon. Edelman and her colleagues refer to this phenomenon as a process that tended to "managerialize" corporate conceptions of cultural and demographic difference, redefining the phenomenon in terms that are more cultural and organizational than legal, and thus more firmly under management's ability to control.

Second, the Edelman et al. study further shows how the diversity construct often harbors a disquieting message: one that defines the value of social differences largely in terms of their instrumental or market value. Paradigmatic here are the passages that are strewn throughout the managerial literature that define diversity as a business necessity, rather than a matter of morality or social justice. Three examples will perhaps suffice:

> It is now a fact that by the year 2000, the workforce will be dominated by groups, such as women and minorities, which traditionally have been discriminated against . . . The bottom line lesson is straightforward: those organizations seen as hostile to (or perhaps merely not supportive of) disenfranchised groups simply will not be able to acquire the competent work force they need to do successful work in the business arena in the next century.

> "Managing diversity" is fast becoming the corporate watchword of the decade – not because corporations are becoming kinder and gentler toward culturally diverse groups but because they want to survive.

> While society has not succeeded in producing a true melting pot, employers have no choice [but to do so]. It is not a question of political correctness; it is a matter of survival . . . Simply put, there are not enough white males to fill all of

the jobs available in the American economy. (Edelman et al.
2001: 1614)

The message implied here is that diversity is a reluctant
accommodation to cultural difference – that is, a development that must be embraced, however begrudgingly, out of a
sheer survival imperative. In all, not a friendly or hospitable
message to historically excluded groups.

And, indeed, there is reason to believe that messages such
as these do inform the workplace arrangements within which
white and minority workers are employed. Perhaps the most
in-depth study along these lines can be found in the ethnographic research conducted by the Harvard organizational
scholars Robin Ely and David Thomas. These authors found,
ironically enough, that the concept of diversity can itself
assume a diverse array of forms. In the most market-driven
business establishment – a bank seeking to extend its business
into minority neighborhoods – management defined diversity
along precisely the lines that the Edelman study laments.
Employees of color were welcomed into the firm – but their
contribution was chiefly defined as an asset with which to win
business from minority neighborhoods. African-American
employees were exclusively assigned to the bank's Retail
Operations division (which served largely African-American
neighborhoods). This had adverse consequences for the
careers of the minority employees, and tethered the careers
of sales personnel to a single customer constituency. A subtle
form of race-typing or ethnic matching thus began to inform
the firm's personnel decisions. In more symbolic or cultural
terms, this conception of diversity also meant that "blacks in
Retail Operations were invited to use their cultural identity,
but only at the boundaries between the organization and its
black market" (Ely and Thomas 2001: 245). This development mirrors the pattern reported in research conducted by
the University of Illinois sociologist Sharon Collins (1997),
who found that firms often encouraged black managers and
executives to adapt their careers to suit the corporate pursuit
of legitimacy with potential minority clientele.

Are these exceptional instances? Perhaps. Ely and Thomas
do unearth several distinct conceptions of diversity, not all
of which tend to perpetuate implicitly racialized organiza-

tional practices. Yet there is good reason to suspect that the corporate pursuit of diversity is often less beneficial than it may seem. For one thing, a large body of research in the sociology of organizations has found that organizational innovations of various types often constitute largely symbolic affirmations of normative ideals. As such, they are more strongly oriented toward external audiences rather than toward the firm's internal operations. Additionally, the recent studies of US diversity practices conducted by Berkeley sociologist Alexandra Kalev and her colleagues (Kalev, Dobbin, and Kelly 2006; Dobbin 2009) have found several revealing points in this connection. Apart from affirmative action programs (which are often mandatory for large firms and government contractors), the most popular corporate diversity practices are those that target the individual biases of managers, typically through diversity training (a practice adopted by more than 40 percent of all US business establishments, about twice the prevalence of more structurally oriented practices). Yet, by tracking the consequences of diversity training over time, Kalev et al. found that diversity training has generally little or no effect on the odds that management jobs will become more demographically inclusive. Indeed, in the case of African-American women and men, the adoption of diversity training actually *reduced* the odds of admission into managerial jobs. Kalev et al. are unable to identify the social processes that account for this pattern, but it does fit well with previous research indicating that corporate conceptions of diversity can erect a protective, legitimacy-oriented shield around the firm – a kind of "exoskeleton" – that either fails to enhance inter-group relations within the firm itself, or else actually exacerbates long-held stereotypes or resentments held by privileged groups (Kalev, Dobbin, and Kelly 2006: 595).

Acknowledging this point, MIT sociologist Emilio Castilla (2008; Castilla and Benard 2010) has conducted research on the phenomenon he terms "the paradox of meritocracy" – that is, the pattern in which firms seeking to base their personnel evaluations on strictly meritocratic criteria "can actually increase ascriptive bias and reduce equity in the workplace" (2008: 1479; emphasis added). Using both survey and experimental methods, Castilla finds that firms that publicly emphasize their use of progressive, merit-based criteria when making personnel evaluations often inadvertently open the door to judgments that are demonstrably biased against historically excluded groups. Whether because managers in such firms develop heightened confidence in their own judgmental powers, or because these firms are emboldened by the "moral credentials" they enjoy, the result is the same: weak or ambiguously formulated conceptions of diversity can have unanticipated consequences, actually freeing managers to act in ways that are at odds with the ideal of an open and inclusive workplace.

The danger is that some of the most popular corporate practices seem either to paper over significant fault lines within the workplace – "diluting diversity," as Linnehan and Konrad (1999) put it – or to narrow the contributions of minority employees, thereby reaffirming the very racial boundaries diversity-minded firms claim to transcend. Perhaps this is why industrial and organizational psychologists find that the pursuit of demographic diversity yields such disappointing results. Indeed, research conducted in a wide array of settings – for example, psychiatric hospitals, high-technology companies, and textile and apparel firms – has found that demographic diversity is often *inversely* proportional to group cohesion, the quality of decision-making, and the dissemination of information across work groups and departments (Lichtenstein et al. 1997; Knight et al. 1999; Townsend and Scott 2001). Again, this suggests that corporate efforts to celebrate our diversity are rather superficial and premature.

To make these points is hardly to question the larger goal of fostering an open and inclusive workplace that eliminates ascriptive inequalities entirely. To the contrary: it is to suggest that corporate practices have adopted forms that are simultaneously too narrow and too broad. Too narrow, in that the diversity construct has often been rigidly tethered to the pursuit of public legitimacy, with profit-making in mind. Too broad, in that the conceptual coordinates of the diversity construct have often been expanded so broadly as to generate ambiguity regarding precisely what diversity means. More structurally attuned approaches, that are firmly rooted in the situation of historically excluded groups, are likely to prove more opportune, much as Kalev, Dobbin, and Kelly (2006) and Dobbin (2009) contend.

Conclusion

Enough has been said in this and in the previous chapter to communicate something of the energy and determination that social scientists have brought to bear on the study of ascriptive inequalities. This is indeed one area where social science research has legal and political resonance, and where it can provoke public debate and deliberation about the structure of opportunity within our society. Yet much remains unknown. For one thing, as scholars have repeatedly noted, it is extremely difficult to identify the precise mechanisms that underlie the disparities that research commonly unearths (Reskin and Padavic 2003). This is especially true with highly quantitative studies, which can disentangle the associations among gender, race, and various types of job rewards, yet must almost always *in*directly infer the sources of the disparities involved. Moreover, most of the research in this vein has been concerned with pay levels, access to promotions, or employee selection as such – a kind of "states and rates" approach that too often neglects the informal boundaries that arise at work, and that often exert subtle yet powerful influences over the course of workers' careers. Further, a gulf has often arisen between social-scientific studies of unequal treatment and the legal criteria and logics used by judicial institutions. Social scientists often bemoan the sociological naivety evident in judicial rulings, which often misconstrue the evidence submitted during litigation. Yet the reverse is also true: sociologists are commonly ignorant of the legal institutions that govern workers' rights and the ways in which social research can usefully inform legal struggles for workers' rights. Only now is research beginning to emerge to fill this gap (Nelson and Bridges 1999; Skaggs 2008).

A final development has also unfolded only recently: the recognition that the workings of gender and racial inequality cannot be understood in isolation from one another. Rather, these two axes of inequality and subordination are commonly conjoined in highly complex ways that defy any efforts to study them separately (Browne and Misra 2003). Studies of wage levels, the exercise of authority at work, and of the status hierarchies that develop within work organizations are beginning to capture these realities, generating what promises to be a truer and more nuanced account of ascriptive inequalities (McCall 2001).

6
The Globalization of Work

Consider this thought experiment for a moment. The year is 1975, and you are asked to identify where the various objects in your environment have been produced. You inspect the various labels on your clothing, furniture, appliances, and even your food. Then you fast-forward to the present, repeating the same exercise. What differences would you find? Who would have produced the material goods that make up everyday life in the earlier year, where, and under what conditions? And what changes would have occurred in the ensuing years?

These are not questions that a consumer-driven society encourages us to ask. Few retailers selling Prada handbags or Dolce & Gabbana shoes would care to invite questions about the working conditions that lie behind such exquisite goods. Yet if we *did* trace the origins of material objects in this way, we would very likely find compelling evidence of a dramatic change that has engulfed many production processes, with far-reaching effects on modern social life. For virtually all artifacts that now surround us in our daily lives – the clothing on our bodies, the furniture and appliances we use, the electronics that bemuse us, the food we eat, and even many services on which we rely – reflect the fact that economic activity has increasingly outgrown national boundaries, generating elaborate webs of commerce that can no longer be contained within nation-states or even whole continents.

Of course, modern capitalism has always been global in its orientation. Yet it is equally true that, during the last quarter-century, the integration of the world's economies has sharply accelerated.[1] Where once a firm and its suppliers might easily have confined their activities to a single metropolitan area or nation, now global production networks reach across oceans, assuming complex, multilayered forms that defy both under-standing and regulation. As activists in the anti-sweatshop movement have argued, the very structure of these produc-tion networks induces firms to violate even the most basic of human rights at work.

Indeed, side by side with the globalization of work there has occurred a steady stream of reports of industrial atrocities in one form or another. Reports of child labor in Indonesia rocked the Nike Corporation throughout the 1990s, leading its CEO to declare, in an outburst of reflexivity, that Nike "has become synonymous with slave wages, forced over-time and arbitrary abuse" (quoted in Cushman 1998). Corporations in the garment industry publicly worried about the risk of "sweatshop stigma" (Bartley and Child 2007, unpublished ms). As well they should: in April 2010, the executives of the retail store H & M were dismayed to learn that a deadly fire had engulfed another of their suppliers' factories in Bangladesh, and that (following the contractor's practice), the workers had all been locked inside. Apple has had massive success with its iPhone and iPad releases – but less admirable are the recent reports that working conditions at its contractor's plant are so abysmal that 12 of its workers committed suicide in the year 2010 alone. (This fact has inspired YouTube postings that tweak Apple's well-known TV advertising campaign, now boasting that "I'm a Mac . . . and I've Got a Dirty Secret.") Finally, reports have brought to light a disturbing point about the production of the circuit boards and transducers that are found in virtually all our electronics: to secure an important raw material used in their production, manufacturers such as Nokia include in their supply chain Congolese and Rwandan warlords, who use slave labor to fuel their mining interests (Smith and Mantz 2006).

It would be comforting to think that these reports are limited to conditions far removed from our own shores. But, as numerous studies of apparel production in the United States have shown, this assumption seems unwarranted. From the 1990s onwards, a steady stream of reports began to surface involving garment factories producing for well-known labels and stores (Liz Claiborne, The Gap, Nike, GUESS? jeans), yet under the most unsavory of conditions. In August 1995, US newspapers reported on the notorious case at El Monte, California, in which several dozen Thai immigrant garment workers had been held in slavery, working 18 hours a day at gunpoint and behind barbed wire (Su, in Ross 1997: 143). Nor were these isolated anecdotes (Collins 2003: ch. 1). According to US government reports, the *majority* of the garment factories in the United States routinely stand in violation of multiple wage, hour, and labor standards laws – the government's definition of a sweatshop (Bonacich and Appelbaum 2000).

Until very recently, interest in globalization was limited to a handful of financial analysts and policymakers who are expert in trade regulations and the flow of currency. By the late 1990s, however, the issue of globalization had exploded onto the public horizon, most dramatically perhaps at the World Trade Organization meetings in Seattle during the fall of 1999. For it was there that the ministers and trade officials of the major world powers met to discuss whether the rules governing trade should be tied to human rights and environmental concerns (the WTO said no). Seeming to embody the very image of institutionalized arrogance, the ministers then found themselves confronted by hundreds of thousands of protesters – union leaders, human rights activists, environmentalists, feminists – who fervently argued against the very conception of global capitalism that the WTO sought to advance. When street clashes ensued and the police forcibly intervened, hundreds of arrests resulted. The debate over globalization had begun in earnest.

Make no mistake: this is not an academic debate; the stakes are high, and the different camps have dug in their heels. For the outcome of the debate over economic globalization will have a crucial impact on the nature of work in virtually all regions of the world (including the advanced capitalist economies in the global North). It has already begun to sensitize consumers in the advanced capitalist nations to the nature of the working conditions under which even the most elegant of consumer goods are produced. As the debate proceeds, it is likely to determine whether the production networks that drive global capitalism can be held accountable to the workers, communities, and nations whose resources they employ. Put simply, it is certainly possible to be uninterested in the details of globalization. But it is no longer possible to be unaffected by them.

This chapter, then, will survey current theory and research on economic globalization. It begins with an analysis of the institutional shifts that opened the way to the globalization of capitalist production (a topic that brings us deep into debates over neo-liberalism). It then assesses arguments that advocates and critics have advanced with respect to the consequences of globalization for workers in various parts of the world, together with evidence addressing these warring claims. The chapter closes by considering a few of the efforts that have been made to protect workers against some of the most harsh and egregious features of global capitalism.

Neo-liberalism: The Cult of the Marketplace

After the end of World War II, the United States enjoyed a position of virtually unchallenged economic power. Yet the situation facing the USA was complex. The world had weathered a massive economic downturn in the 1930s, and then suffered the convulsions that generated the Holocaust and a devastating world war. The task of rebuilding the Western world, of stabilizing the world economy, and avoiding disruptive economic crises was simply too massive for any single nation to address. It was for this reason that the major Western powers established inter-governmental bodies that could provide much-needed sources of international stability and predictability. The major institutions set up to accomplish these tasks were the World Bank and the International Monetary Fund. The former was charged with helping to fund the reconstruction of Western Europe and to develop the former colonial nations (many of whom, such as India, had just won their independence with the end of the war). The latter was charged with helping to ensure that the international economy avoided financial crises of the sort that brought about the Great Depression of the 1930s.

There were, of course, policy debates among the Western powers that governed the IMF and the World Bank. US economists often embraced a doctrine known as "modernization theory," which sought to project American economic thinking onto much of the developing world. Yet, following the economic orthodoxy of the day, the IMF and World Bank defined their mission on the basis of Keynesian economic policies: the IMF sought to ensure that sufficient levels of aggregate demand existed whenever circumstances required; in this way, major banking crises and other financial catastrophes could be avoided (usually through the making of emergency loans and extensions of credit as need be). For its part, the World Bank helped to approve and fund major programs of structural development – major investment programs that promised to develop the economic capacity of the developing world.

By the late 1970s, the theoretical orthodoxy that economists embraced had begun to shift, partly in response to events unfolding in various parts of the world. For one thing, Western corporations had begun to face growing limits on their profitability, largely because of the power of labor unions and political parties. Social movements in the developing world had also emerged, providing cause for concern regarding corporate profitability – first in parts of the Middle East (as in Iran in the 1950s), and then in Latin America (Guatemala in the 1950s, the Dominican Republic in the 1960s, and Chile in the early 1970s). The net effect, coupled with concerns about economic performance of the largest capitalist enterprises, led many economists and world leaders to conclude that new approaches toward economic policy were needed if the economic order was to develop in the most advantageous way.

With the elections first of Margaret Thatcher in Great Britain, and then of Ronald Reagan in the United States, there emerged a major reconfiguration of the policies and practices that the IMF and World Bank used to govern the world economy. What emerged – first in the most powerful nations, through programs of de-regulation and privatization, and then on the international scene – were policies and doctrines advocating an ever-greater reliance on the marketplace as the sole mechanism governing the allocation of goods and services. Public provision of goods – whether through social insurance programs, subsidies to industry, or barriers to trade – came to be viewed as obstacles to economic development. They were to be uprooted wherever possible.

Essentially, the vision of economic development that the IMF and World Bank embraced sought to restore the free trade (or "liberal") economic policies that had shaped capitalism up until the 1930s. The onset of the Great Depression, of course, compelled nations to depart from liberal or laissez-faire doctrines, embracing Keynesian strategies that used the public sector as a means of managing or stabilizing economic growth. By the end of the Vietnam War, though, economic stagnation compelled policymakers to seek out alternative paths. In so doing, they gravitated toward the ideas of such deeply conservative thinkers as Friederich von Hayek and Milton Friedman, who advocated a return to laissez-faire policies. Hence the "neo-liberal" name that has been widely used to describe the new orthodoxy governing social and economic life. Derided by its critics as "market fundamentalism," neo-liberalism advocates the privatization of virtually all economic activity, including the provision of goods and services that have traditionally been channeled through public sources. The notion here is a radical one: government intervention can only introduce inefficiencies and distortions into systems that are best left in private hands. The market is the best means of governing virtually all social life.

The origins of neo-liberal thinking are only now beginning to come to light. According to research by the economic sociologist Johanna Bockman (Bockman and Bernstein 2008), one important source of neo-liberal theory stemmed from the Eastern Bloc nations, where intellectuals experimented with market logics as a means of weakening the grip of communist parties on their societies. Ironically, their theories proved useful to policymakers in the Western capitalist nations, who increasingly aimed neo-liberal doctrine at the welfare state, at socialist governments in the developing world (as with the overthrow of the Allende regime in Chile), and at powerful labor unions (as under the Thatcher government in the UK). Neo-liberal rhetoric (though not necessarily its practices) found its most prominent platform with the ascent to power of the Reagan administration. Indeed, by the early 1980s, neo-liberal policies were so widely shared among elite economic policymakers that they came to be called the "Washington Consensus." Neo-liberalism has provided the dominant paradigm through which economic activity is understood, both within the developing and developed world alike.

Application of neo-liberal policies to the less developed countries (LDCs) has often involved wrenchingly painful and coercive economic measures. Applying the new doctrine, the IMF has often provided financial credits or loans to nations facing crises, but only on the condition that the receiving nation make massive "structural adjustments" in return, slashing public expenditures, privatizing all nationalized industries, imposing tight monetary policies that dramatically devalue workers' wages, de-regulating all economic sectors, and eliminating trade barriers that protected domestic industries from foreign corporations. This approach has often amounted to a kind of "shock treatment" – the effects of which have been sharply debated for a quarter-century now.

These were not minor shifts, or simply the preferences of a few bureaucrats with offices in Washington, DC. For, with the opening up of China to capitalist economic activity, and with the fall of the Eastern Bloc nations, neo-liberal policies have managed to insinuate themselves into every corner of the world. With some minor exceptions, the international economic system has been placed on a new footing, and large transnational corporations have come to enjoy almost unlimited space within which to operate. Neo-liberalism, in other words, has defined the new rules of the game.

This change dramatically reoriented the economic policies on which LDCs had relied up to that point. For the strategies that developing nations used (often at the behest of the IMF) invoked "import-substitution" strategies for industrialization. The notion here is simple: rather than buying goods from foreign suppliers – a practice that allowed revenues to flow to the selling country, and prevented the LDC from developing its own productive capacity – LDCs erected strong trade barriers with which to favor domestic production. This increased the price of imported goods (for example, on

machinery or consumer goods), but it gave domestic producers some desperately needed breathing room, allowing them
to gain their footing without being overwhelmed by more
powerful economies. Now, however, with the ascent of neo-
liberal policies, societies throughout the developing world
were expected – and financial aid was conditioned on their
willingness – to adopt "export-oriented" strategies for industrialization. Less developed countries would be expected to
open their markets up, to remove the trade barriers that had
sheltered home industry, and to allow unrestricted foreign
investment into their economies. In other words, LDCs
were expected to succeed by enacting economic reforms that
integrated them more fully into the markets of the global
capitalist order – an economy that was dominated by large
transnational corporations.

The consequences have been massive for societies around
the world. For one thing, it was the opening up of markets
within the developing world that made it possible and desirable for the largest corporations to relocate substantial parts of
their business operations overseas. This has encouraged what
some analysts have called the "hyper-mobility" of capital:
the ability of business establishments to relocate production
wherever an advantageous locale could be found. Although
this raises complex issues about the causes of de-industrialization and the dismantling of manufacturing establishments
in the United States, there can be no doubt that the advent of
neo-liberal policies governing trade and financial intervention
acted to encourage a shift of US manufacturing operations
to foreign platforms, whether to the Mexican *maquilado-
ras* or to Export Processing Zones (EPZs) in Asia and Latin
America. Even the possibility of such factory relocations has
cast a chill on the nature of labor relations in much of the
advanced capitalist world (as we discuss further below).

Even more pronounced, however, have been the changes
that have unfolded in the developing world, as policies for
economic development have recast social and economic life.
This can perhaps be seen most clearly in the rapid growth
of EPZs throughout the developing world. Essentially, these
are spatially defined areas of a developing society where
economic transactions receive especially favorable conditions, such as the suspension of labor laws, tax policies,

minimum wage laws and even workers' citizenship rights. Critics deride EPZs, viewing them as "rights-free" spaces that provide generous profits for transnational corporations with no enduring benefit for the host nation. Advocates suggest that EPZs eventually do provide benefits in the form of jobs and economic growth for nations that would otherwise have neither. What cannot be debated is the rapid proliferation of these zones. According to ILO data, in 1975 there were only 79 EPZs scattered among 25 countries in the world. A decade later, the number of EPZs had doubled, and by 1996 that number had increased to 845 zones located in 93 nations. In 2006, the number of EPZs had grown to 3,500, and were located in 130 nations around the world. Roughly 66 million workers are employed in these zones; two thirds of these workers labor in the Special Economic Zones established in various parts of China, while substantial numbers are also employed in Central America and Mexico (Boyenga 2007).

China's experience with its Special Economic Zones, though surely not emblematic, commands particular attention here. Many of the SEZs are located in rapidly growing industrial cities, such as Shenzhen and Xiamen in Guangdong province, on the coast of the South China Sea. As is true of many SEZs, Shenzhen's is surrounded by a gate, and requires official permission to enter. The SEZs are enmeshed in a regional web in which finance capital and high-tech centers radiating outward from Taiwan, Shanghai, and Hong Kong utilize the South China Sea as a rapidly growing industrial base. One of the keys to their rapid growth is suggested by the Berkeley anthropologist Aihwa Ong, who points out that, unlike workers employed within state enterprises as such, workers in the SEZs

> are considered peasants unprotected by China's labor laws and are not entitled to social benefits due workers elsewhere in the country . . . As rural migrants, they are not entitled to urban citizenship and the residential rights, education for their children, and access to various subsidies that such citizenship entails. The massive influx of the "floating population," much of it young and female, supplies the SEZs with cheap labor for huge factories producing consumer goods for the global economy. (2006: 106)

Almost all of the SEZs depend heavily for their labor sources on young female workers. Presumably, in labor-intensive operations, women are preferred because of the significantly lower wages they receive, and the greater institutional controls to which they can be subjected (Ngai and Smith 2007; Nichols et al. 2004; Lee 1998).

It is important to understand the nature of the work that has emerged within factories in China's economic zones. Especially helpful in this respect is the brilliant ethnography by Pun Ngai, *Made in China: Women Factory Workers in a Global Workplace* (2005). Pun worked and lived for the better part of a year at Meteor Electronics, a Hong Kong-owned electronics plant in Szenzhen that produced GPS devices for use in upscale German cars. As is typical, the overwhelming majority of Pun's subjects were young single women who had migrated from rural regions scattered throughout Southern China. At Meteor, they encountered a powerful system of social control that provided the factory with three overlapping sources of power over their labor: the capitalist labor process; the patriarchal kinship systems that remain pervasive in many parts of China; and the Chinese state itself.

In Pun's account, the capitalist labor process is deeply despotic; it subjects workers to elaborate penalties for even minor infractions, and exposes them to a sophisticated form of Taylorism that uses video surveillance to enforce labor discipline. Workers must secure "out of position" permits to use the bathroom, and are often peppered with insulting descriptions of them as uncivilized, ignorant, and uneducated (owing to their rural origins). Patriarchal family relations impinge on women's working lives in many respects, perhaps most importantly by defining their employment as a temporary affiliation that can last only until they assume a role more in keeping with their fundamental obligation – that of marrying and having children. As Pun observes, these factory women are popularly known as *dagongmei* ("working daughters"), implying that their work roles are subordinate to their gender. Moreover, *dagongmei* are often recruited into their jobs through kinship networks, thus further obliging them to labor dutifully on behalf of their kin.

The third source of power to which these workers are subjected stems from the post-socialist state apparatus, which is well articulated with capital's needs and with the patriarchal relations that exist within China. As Ong mentions, China's population registry system (*hukou*) roots workers' rights in their place of birth, and thus defines these workers as non-citizens, both in the plant and in its surrounding community. Their status is therefore limited to that of contract workers who are only temporarily residents of the city in which they work. Indeed, their right to live within Shenzhen is conferred only on the basis of their employment; should they be fired or quit, their residency permits would be nullified. Moreover, because they lack settlement rights and are therefore not eligible for local housing, they are compelled to live within the company's dormitories (Ngai and Smith 2007; Nichols et al. 2004). Ngai observes:

> The *hukou* system helps to create exploitative mechanisms of labor appropriation in Shenzhen as well as other cities in China . . . The *hukou* system, mixed with labor control, is the specific modality of power that makes up the ambiguous identity of the rural migrant labor and deepens, but at the same time obscures, their exploitation. Are the temporary residents treated as urban residents or not? Are the temporary workers regarded as workers or as peasants? The answers to these questions are always ambiguous. (2005: 46)

The ambiguity of the workers' status – half peasant, half worker – is only compounded by the elaborate, hierarchical system of contracts that Pun reports, which assigns workers contracts of different lengths, depending on their rank. Because of their liminal, migrant status, "places for migrant workers to organize themselves as a class force are wiped out" (ibid.: 48).

The image that Pun develops is one in which global capital has, with the help of the Chinese post-socialist state, located an especially pliant and cheap source of labor in the Special Economic Zones. The *dagongmei*, subjected to a powerful structural nexus of control, provide a nearly endless river of willing workers, many of whom are enticed by the excitement of modern urban life. Their sojourning mentality becomes all the more convenient for the factory managers, since it institutionalizes a form of turnover that minimizes the dangers of industrial conflict. For hundreds of millions of workers (often young and female), whether in China, the Dominican Republic, or in Bangladesh, this is the face of global capitalism.

Globalization: The Debate

The question, of course, ultimately hinges on the effects that global capitalism is likely to have on workers in the developing and the developed world alike. Will neo-liberalism eventually strengthen the developing economies, generating a measure of prosperity and perhaps even an expansion of workers' rights? Or will market relations have a harsher effect, compelling workers to compete against one another, fueling a "race to the bottom"? And must the growth of the developing world come at the expense of the advanced capitalist economies? How will the various classes in the affluent North fare in the wake of globalization?

The champions of neo-liberal reforms and the global integration they advocate have made a series of arguments that we do well to consider. Key here is the role of foreign direct investment, which occurs when transnational corporations build production facilities overseas, or otherwise develop a direct ownership stake in business activity abroad. Advocates of neo-liberal policies argue that the presence of transnational corporations overseas tends to produce a "demonstration effect" – that is, to establish norms and practices that over time tend to favor the rule of law and the furtherance of democratic institutions. Further, advocates of global integration contend that TNCs generally provide higher wages and better working conditions than do local businesses, thus raising labor standards, whether directly or indirectly, in ways that ripple throughout the host nation's economy. Moreover, the hope is that by adopting an export-oriented approach toward economic growth, LDCs can accumulate reserves of foreign currency and gain business skills and expertise that will equip their business establishments to move upward in the global chain, developing manufacturing and even design capacities that they could not otherwise acquire. Or so the argument goes.

And no one has made this argument more forcefully than the Columbia University economist Jagdish Bhagwati, whose 2004 *In Defense of Globalization* provides something of a manifesto in support of the neo-liberal view. Bhagwati views the critics of structural reform as largely well intended but hopelessly naive about the actual operations of economic activities around the world. He mobilizes a wealth of economic studies in support of several sweeping claims: that economic integration increases wages and reduces levels of poverty throughout the developing world; that it leads in the direction of greater gender equality; and that it tends to eliminate child labor and expand workers' rights. Moreover, he argues that efforts to defend the position of workers in LDCs commonly have unanticipated consequences that can actually harm the very workers they seek to help. He claims, for example, that US legislation against child labor in the early 1990s had the perverse effect of shutting factories in Bangladesh almost overnight, throwing Bengali families into desperate economic straits and often forcing them to sell their female children into prostitution (2004: 71). Bhagwati defends Export Processing Zones – the "rights-free" regions mentioned above – suggesting that, as developing countries "begin to gradually shift to an export orientation," the operational success of these zones penetrates into all sectors of the economy. As examples, he cites the often-touted example of the East Asian economies (the various "tigers" of Malaysia, Singapore, Taiwan, and South Korea), whose export-oriented strategies generated levels of growth during the 1970s and 1980s that sharply outpaced that of India, which remained closed to structural reforms until the 1990s.

Perhaps the most audacious of Bhagwati's claims involve the impact of the EPZs on gender inequalities. Refuting arguments about the greater vulnerability of women to exploitation and abuse in these low-wage, labor-intensive jobs, Bhagwati goes so far as to emphasize the emancipatory effect of such employment. Citing a study of garment factories in Bangladesh, he argues that, here, women workers do "endure onerous working conditions, but they also experience pride in their earnings, maintain a higher standard of dress than their unemployed counterparts and, most significantly, develop an identity apart from being a child or wife," and often experience a "degree of autonomy, self-respect, and freedom from traditional gender work" that they would not enjoy in the absence of free market practices (Bhagwati 2004: 85).

Another prominent advocate of neo-liberal policies has been Nicholas Kristof, the Pulitzer Prize winning correspondent for the *New York Times*. Generally admired for his courageous coverage of human rights atrocities in Africa and other parts of the world, Kristof has criticized anti-sweatshop activists and other opponents of structural reform, arguing that such efforts represent a misguided imposition of the rich world's concerns onto populations whose needs are simply different from what affluent activists assume. Kristof struck these themes in 2000, while co-authoring a larger project about the rise of the Asian economies. In his 2000 essay, "Two Cheers for Sweatshops" (*New York Times*: September 24), for example, Kristof viewed even the most desperately harsh and low-wage manufacturing jobs as a route upward from abject destitution: "For all the misery they can engender, sweatshops at least offer a precarious escape from the poverty that is the developing world's greatest problem." Later, Kristof explained: "My point is that as bad as sweatshops are, the alternatives are worse. They are more dangerous, lower-paying, and more degrading" (*New York Times*: January 14, 2009). By boycotting US retailers that employ low-wage labor in the developing world, he concluded, solidarity movements wind up depriving developing nations of the only asset they have: their capacity to provide cheap labor. "The only thing a country like Cambodia has to offer is terribly cheap wages; if countries are scolded for paying those wages, they will shift their manufacturing to marginally richer areas like Malaysia or Mexico" (ibid.).

What can be said about these arguments in favor of the neo-liberal model? This is not the place to attempt anything resembling a full discussion of economic policy and developmental strategies. Yet, within the limits of the present context, it seems clear that the advocates of economic integration greatly oversimplify highly complex realities, and trivialize the very real dangers that structural reforms often impose on the developing world. First, the relation between trade openness and wages in the developing world is in many respects far more complex (and less uniformly advantageous) than Bhagwati et al. allow. The short-term effect of adopting an open, export-oriented economic strategy is often to reduce workers' wages, as labor-intensive factories find it necessary to engage in a "race to the bottom" as a condition of renewing contracts with prestigious retailers. In a study conducted for the World Bank, for example, Martin Rama cites studies of Mexico and Uruguay, where "workers in protected sectors enjoy higher wages and better working conditions than their counterparts in sectors exposed to foreign competition" (2003: 13). Second, the beneficial effects of foreign direct investment often seem to fade after two or three years, as local conditions overwhelm any demonstration effect. Third, since IMF and World Bank policies often impose stern conditions on developing nations seeking capital for investment purposes (the "structural adjustments" that often amount to shock therapy), the consequences can mean massive layoffs for large sectors of the labor force who were employed in governmental jobs or state-owned enterprises. These workers then begin a downward economic trajectory (especially among women workers) that the advocates of neo-liberal policies tend to neglect. Fourth, the risks of integration within the global economy are overwhelming. Given that developing nations often compete in the same low-wage industries, the danger of over-production in particular commodity markets, correlative price declines, and economic crises are often quite real.

The need for a nuanced understanding of the consequences of neo-liberal policies emerges in a series of careful studies conducted by social scientists who have scrutinized the impact of the EPZs on economic development. Much of this work examines the degree to which LDCs really *are* able to climb up the value chain, moving from vulnerable positions as suppliers of cheap exports to more autonomous positions as manufacturers of increasingly capital-intensive goods. Their findings are instructive.

The University of Pittsburgh political scientist Nita Rudra (2005) finds that globalization (measured by the importance of manufacturing exports for a nation's output) has contradictory effects on the labor market positions of workers in the developing world. Examining trends from 1972 to 1997, she finds that integration in the global economy enhances the labor market position of workers in more affluent parts of the developing world (such as Korea), but that it tends to weaken the position of workers in poorer nations (such as Indonesia or the Philippines). The University of North Carolina political scientist Layna Mosley and her colleagues have found broadly similar results. Using a unique data set that tracks shifts in violations of workers' rights in 90 developing nations from 1986 to 2002, Mosley and Uno (2007) find that openness to trade tends to bring about an erosion of workers' rights over time. Foreign Direct Investment (FDI), however, had the opposite effect, instead enhancing workers' rights. Mosely has not broken down the distinct effects that flow from FDI within export processing zones, however, and thus differences that flow from the *types* of FDI remain unexamined in her study.

Finally, the dangers of neo-liberal reforms are made apparent in an important series of studies conducted by University of New Mexico sociologist Andrew Schrank (2001, 2004). Schrank examines an important argument that advocates of neo-liberalism often make: that by adopting EPZs, nations can climb upward in the value chain, moving from low-wage production work in labor-intensive industries such as simple assembly of garments, to higher-wage work in capital-intensive plants ("full package manufacturing"). Studying several cases in Central America and the Caribbean, Schrank finds several reasons to question the rosy predictions that advocates often make. First, the returns to "full package manufacturing" are far less frequent than predicted, and often restricted to nations with substantial domestic markets (making them worthwhile targets of investment by transnational corporations). Second, nations that adopt the "full-package" model often find that *other* nations have often done so as well, thus creating real dangers of over-production. Finally, nations seeking to climb upward in the value chain tend to experience resistance from transnational corporations, who are loathe to tolerate aggressive competition from upstart manufacturers (as when firms in the developing world seek to establish independent branding). There are numerous forces that confront developing nations with the danger of embracing what Kaplinsky (2001) referred to as "industrial monoculture" – economic models whose gains prove less sustainable and risky than they seem at first glance.

Implied in the arguments of these critics can be found a distinctly different conception of the structure and operation of global capitalism. The notion here is that however well-intended might be the managers and executives of transnational corporations, they face structural imperatives and constraints on their actions that have consequences for the nature of work in both the developed and developing world. One of the most important considerations here is the increasing reliance by TNCs on elaborate supply chains in lieu of direct ownership of production facilities (Castells 1996; Reich 1991).[2] Any given supply chain is organized in a complex hierarchical fashion. Lead firms at the top – those which are responsible for the design and sales of the finished product – contract with suppliers for the production and assembly of component parts. Doing this may require negotiations with dozens or even hundreds of independent firms, agents, shippers, and other middlemen, each of whom maintains its own network of suppliers and contractors. At the bottom of the chain are small producers who may employ workers on a job-lot basis and who must therefore accept whatever terms are offered in any contract. In any given supply chain, lead firms capture a disproportionate share of the value added, reflecting their control over design, branding, or retail chain outlets. And because they face sharp global competition at each level in the chain, firms continually press their suppliers to cut their production costs to the bone. The further down in the chain one looks, the more ferocious such cost-cutting pressures tend to be.

Surely the purest expression of how this structure works is that of Walmart, the single largest corporation in the world. So massive is Walmart's presence in the global economy that its imports from China account for roughly 10 percent of the US trade deficit with that nation. Walmart maintains its home procurement headquarters in Shenzhen, China, near the Pearl River Delta, which serves as the base from which it negotiates contracts with its Chinese suppliers. Their relationship is revealing. As Bonacich and Wilson put it:

> Wal-Mart's procurement staff members are constantly making deals with hundreds of Chinese manufacturers on a daily basis

in order to produce goods tailored to Wal-Mart's own stringent specifications; these include pricing, quality assurance,
efficiency, and delivery. Wal-Mart is also known to demand
that its suppliers change their bookkeeping systems and
improve their logistics to meet rigid delivery schedules while
maintaining the lowest price margins. In exchange for Wal-
Mart contracts, Chinese companies are often required to open
up their books to Wal-Mart and cut prices where necessary, if
Wal-Mart decides the supplier's profit margins are too large.
(2008: 29)

Walmart (like many other powerful retailers and sellers of
brand-name merchandise) is, of course, a favorite target for
criticism. But the point here is that firms in its position are
not simply responding to, or accepting, low-wage conditions
in the global economy. To the contrary: they are actively
constituting and diffusing such low standards, and resisting
with equal energy all efforts to change them. As Bonacich
and Wilson note, when Chinese authorities proposed labor
law reforms in October 2006, "the American Chamber of
Commerce in Shanghai, with companies like Wal-Mart and
Nike as members, recorded its fierce objections" (2008: 30).
The reforms, such as they were, were substantially weakened
as a result.

Several implications follow from this structure. First, since
production networks now stretch across national boundaries
and even continents, it becomes almost impossible for any
single nation to exercise regulatory power over the production establishments within its jurisdiction. Production
is increasingly transnational, and corresponding means of
regulating labor regimes have simply not emerged. Moreover,
the global reach of TNCs makes it hard for any single nation
to police the labor standards either on its own territory or
elsewhere, even if it has the institutional capacity. To do so
with any degree of zeal would very likely prompt the firm to
move its operations to more pliant ("competitive") sites. This
hyper-mobility of capital deepens the asymmetrical nature of
the relation between large transnational employers, on the
one hand, and the host nations and workforces they employ,
on the other. Especially where the nation-state is weak, or
where political traditions have fostered authoritarian rule,
competitive pressures established within global supply chains

lead to a proliferation of deeply coercive and abusive forms of employment that routinely deny workers even the most basic of labor standards regarding wages, hours, or safety and health. This is especially true for women workers, who in many cases constitute the vast majority of the manufacturing workforces in the developing world, and (as noted with respect to China's Special Economic Zones) often encounter kinship relationships and government policies that sharply curtail their freedom of movement and ability to claim any civil rights.

By its very nature, economic globalization has effects that transcend any region of the world, affecting workers in the developing and developed world alike, although in very different and uncertain ways. Focusing our attention on the pattern unfolding in the United States, we can examine two analytically separate but closely related aspects of work in an era of global capitalism: first, shifts in the *nature* of the work situations that employees encounter (including everything from the wages and working conditions they face to the balance of power between themselves and the firm). And, second, changes in the *level* of employment within some of the most sought-after jobs in the American economy: high-wage manufacturing jobs, which have undergirded many cities and regions in the United States (especially in the US Midwest). What conclusions can be drawn with respect to these two questions?

Shifts in the nature of employment can perhaps be seen most clearly within industries that have been most directly linked to globalization, such as apparel. This industry has traditionally been a low-wage, labor-intensive branch of the economy marked by few barriers to entry (relatively small amounts of capital are needed to set up shop). This industry has, of course, been a mobile one: historically, the British apparel trade was surpassed by its New England rivals, which in turn experienced the relocation of the industry to the American South. Now, most of the industry's operations have been shifted to Asian and Latin American plants, as discussed above. Yet hundreds of thousands of jobs in this industry (and in textiles and leather goods) are indeed located in the United States, especially in Los Angeles, New York, and the US South, as some retailers favor contractors whose proximity enables them to respond quickly to shifts in fashion and consumer demand. Yet the jobs these contractors provide, which are now held by an overwhelmingly immigrant work-force, have come to resemble those located in the developing world. Indeed, some workers have begun to circulate back and forth between similar garment factories in the US and the Caribbean Basin (Collins 2003; Bonacich and Appelbaum 2000). As was noted at the outset of this chapter, the result has been the resurgence of sweatshops in the United States. In *Behind the Label*, a systematic survey of the Los Angeles garment industry, Edna Bonacich and Richard Appelbaum find that an overwhelming majority of apparel workshops provided labor conditions with serious deficiencies in worker safety and health, with multiple OSHA and Department of Labor violations (2000). This study essentially confirmed what had been reported in government bulletins just a few years earlier, indicating widespread violations of minimum-wage laws (and even non-payment of wages entirely), overwork, and safety and health violations. Jane Collins's *Threads* (2003) connected garment plants in the United States and Latin America, and found that the sharp escalation of cross-border competitive pressures in this industry had led a Virginia plant to assign multiple jobs to individual workers (what had been termed a "stretch-out" in textiles 80 years ago).

The question, of course, is precisely how pervasive these pressures seem to be. Here, several sources of concern are to be found. One stems from the labor regime that Walmart has adopted in the United States. This is not the place to wade into the debate over Walmart's practices – a controversy that has, it seems, become a cottage industry in its own right (Lichtenstein 2006). Here it must suffice to note that a signifi-cant proportion of Walmart's employees must resort to food stamps and Medicaid to survive (with their low wages, many are in fact eligible for public assistance), and that a disturbing number of lawsuits have been filed against the firm, indicat-ing a set of practices "that either evade or outright violate the core laws and standards that govern job quality in the US" (Bernhardt et al. 2008: 2). Given how deeply embedded in the global economy Walmart's operations are, it seems reasonable to conclude that its labor practices are, ironically enough, being imported from its global supply chain. Equally worrisome is the possibility that Walmart's ability to impose a despotic labor regime on its workers has begun to exert "demonstration effects" within the advanced capitalist world, leading to the Walmartization of work in any industry or region where Walmart has a significant market presence – in retail chains that sell groceries, appliances, apparel, electronics, toys, and pharmaceuticals.

That employers have been able to impose such unfavorable terms and conditions of employment on a wide swath of the US labor market raises the second issue warranting attention: the link between *levels* of employment, especially in manufacturing, traditionally a high-wage branch of the economy. This question has, of course, been the subject of heated debate and polemic from all sides of the political spectrum, especially as discussion of the out-sourcing and off-shoring of work exploded into mainstream media. Examples of this polemic include the nightly sequence, *Exporting America*, that the former CNN host Lou Dobbs ran on his evening broadcast, or the raft of books (such as Senator Byron Dorgan's *Take this Job and Ship It* (2006), alleging economic treason on the part of American-based multi-national corporations. Fears that US corporations are sending growing numbers of high-wage jobs to the developing world – most prominently, to China and Mexico – compelled the Chairman for the President's Council of Economic Advisers, Gregory Mankiw, to publicly apologize for his widely reported comments that seemed to favor the outsourcing of American jobs. What is the reality beneath these fears?

Up until the end of the recession of 2000–02, it was still possible for analysts to view the link between globalization and job losses in manufacturing as more spurious than real. Thus, economists could easily point to serious flaws in the nature of widely reported studies of the off-shoring of jobs, providing a measure of reassurance to a worried public. Since the end of that recession, however, several changes have unfolded in the US economy that have ratcheted up the level of concern. In a word, the linkage between globalization and the hemorrhaging of US manufacturing has begun to look increasingly real (see Blinder 2006).

Two facts are important to establish at the outset here.

First, there can be no doubt that this has been a period of a sustained loss of industrial jobs during a time of rapid globalization. Thus, in 1979, just before a major recession, manufacturing employment in the United States peaked at roughly 19.5 million workers. By 2008, on the eve of another and much deeper downturn, the number of manufacturing jobs in the United States had fallen to 10 million workers, or roughly half its previous number (Congressional Budget Office 2008). Second, there are many factors other than globalization – most notably, increases in productivity, changing financial strategies adopted by large corporations, and weakening institutional protections against downsizing – that have contributed to such sharp and sustained job losses. What has been happening in the last decade, however, is that patterns of trade and the operation of the global economy have apparently posed a growing threat to industrial employment located in the United States. Specifically, during the 1999–2007 years, imports of manufactured goods produced abroad have taken a growing "bite" out of US-based production jobs in such industries as apparel, textiles, metals, and machinery, as well as computers and electronics. What is important to note is that a substantial proportion – precisely how much is not known – of imported manufactured goods are in fact produced under contract for US-based firms that have opted to move their production operations to other countries.

Frustrated by the fact that existing data are unable to unpack the movements of US production operations, Cornell labor scholar Kate Bronfenbrenner and her colleagues designed a series of studies that used newspaper reports to track corporate decisions to shift production lines to sites located off-shore (most often, China) or near-shore (Mexico). She found several points that warrant attention (see Bronfenbrenner and Luce 2004). First, the movement of production from high-wage to low-wage countries is a global phenomenon, affecting European as well as US industry. Second, significant changes in out-sourcing have occurred during the last decade. Up to 2001, for example, out-sourcing to China was concentrated in such industries as toys, electronics, and household goods; since then, out-sourcing has grown more widespread, affecting a broader swath of industries and encompassing aerospace, industrial equipment and machinery, and metal fabrication, among others. And, third, even controlling for the disproportionate presence of unions within the manufacturing sector, the results suggest that unionized workplaces stand at particular risk of out-sourcing, especially in the movement of production to China. Finally, it bears mentioning that even the threat of out-sourcing seems to cast a pall over relations between employers and workers. As Bronfenbrenner found in an earlier series of studies (2000), in the years following NAFTA, employers became increasingly likely to threaten to relocate production to overseas (often to Mexico) while bargaining over wages and working conditions. Given these developments, it should not be surprising that Human Rights Watch, describing the state of workers' rights in the United States, wrote in 2000 that "workers' freedom of association is under sustained attack . . . and the government is often failing its responsibility under international human rights standards . . . to protect workers' rights" (in Seidman 2007).

All this would seem to constitute a litany of despair. Yet, as was argued in chapter 3, the structures of work and employment are not driven by economic imperatives alone; social and political influences inevitably intervene, shaping the outcome of economic structures. This is the approach taken by Columbia economic sociologist Josh Whitford (2005). In *The New Old Economy*, Whitford recognizes the depth of the injuries that US industry has suffered at the hands of global competition, and notes the devastating impact these trends have had on the Midwestern states, in particular. In his nuanced analysis of the experience of multiple manufacturing firms in this region, he takes care to point out the multiple successes that have emerged under inhospitable institutional conditions. Drawing on much of the literature on industrial clusters and regional economic growth, Whitford argues that there is indeed a future for high-wage US manufacturing, but that nurturing such outcomes will require economic policies that are far better attuned to the needs of firms in select industries. Especially promising are industries that do not compete on wages or production costs, but on product quality, with engineering innovation. As he notes:

> There are many firms even in the central and historic "rust belt" that *are* somehow groping their way toward the

formation of globally competitive, highly flexible, collaborative production networks ... ; yet at the same time, these
efforts have been contradictory at best and are only weakly
supported by the existing American institutional infrastruc-
ture. (2005: 2)

The question is whether it is possible to override the traditional US aversion to active public intervention, thus
dislodging the reigning neo-liberal policy. At issue is the need
for a coherent industrial policy that might stop the bleeding.

Regulating Global Capitalism: Solidarity Movements and Codes of Conduct

Perhaps one of the most potent assets that global capitalism
wields is its aura of inevitability. In this view, globalization
is an irresistible reality that overwhelms the capacity of well-
meaning citizens and nations. And indeed, as just seen, it is
clear that global production networks have outstripped the
regulatory capacities of any individual nation-state. Yet no
labor regime is invulnerable. And global production networks that supply brand-name goods to prominent retailers
are a case in point. They have created important spaces of
resistance within which transnational social movements have
found it possible to challenge, and potentially to transform,
the labor regimes currently taking shape.

Human rights movements had long targeted governments,
focusing on them either as sources of oppression or as levers
of reform. By the 1990s, however, a broad transnational
movement of activists had begun to develop new strategies
and tactics that reflected the changed terrain in an era of
global capitalism. Given the trans-border nature of so much
economic activity, and the weakness of many governments
in the developing world, activists began to focus their work
on corporate power. Utilizing what Keck and Sikkink (1998)
have called "accountability politics," activists engaged in
efforts at "naming and shaming" prominent corporations
into enforcing specific factory codes of conduct. What gives
these solidarity movements particular momentum is their
ability to target something of special value to large retailers

like Nike, The Gap, or Liz Claiborne: their brand, or "reputational capital," the value of which can easily be threatened by public campaigns that reveal the unsavory practices that exist behind the firm's fashionable commodities (Ross 1997; Esbenshade 2004; Klein 2000).

The transnational groups that arose, such as the United Students Against Sweatshops (USAS), the National Labor Committee (NLC), and the Worker Rights Consortium (WRC), all engaged in energetic campaigns during the 1990s, often aided by religious groups. In 1995, after a long campaign in which NLC activists had exposed egregious conditions at a contractor in El Salvador that supplied The Gap, the retailer agreed to a program of independent monitoring; this was the first such agreement in this context. USAS made major headway with respect to universities, who sought to publicly affirm sweat-free credentials for their paraphernalia. Major corporations and public figures were humiliated, as when it was revealed that the line of clothing marketed by the celebrity Kathie Lee Gifford was produced in a Honduras sweatshop that utilized child labor. Despite this momentum, cracks soon appeared in the anti-sweatshop movement, and sharply divergent approaches soon appeared toward corporate codes and monitoring systems. Key differences centered on the degree of independence of monitors from the retailers whose plants they inspected, whether factory inspections were to be random, and whether practices at any given factory were to be made publicly known. One major group, the Fair Labor Association (FLA), was formed at the behest of the Clinton administration's Department of Labor in 1998. The FLA has succeeded in engaging industry in its efforts, but doing so required major sacrifices in the nature of its program. Rejecting this approach as useless, and fearing that FLA's approach would act merely as a fig leaf, concealing enduring problems in corporate practices, USAS and NLC broke away to form a rival umbrella group, the WRC, which utilizes a far stricter system of corporate codes and monitoring. In addition to these approaches, there has been a proliferation of other systems of codes and monitoring, some of which are advanced by the apparel industry (such as the Worldwide Responsible Apparel Production program), while still others are retailer-specific. The largest of the proprietary systems is maintained by Nike, which conducts annual audits at each of its 800 suppliers (Locke, Qin, and Brause 2007; see also Esbenshade 2004; Rodriguez-Garavito 2005).

There is broad agreement now that the anti-sweatshop movement has begun to lose much of its momentum. There remain deeply committed groups (such as the WRC and the Maquila Solidarity Network), which have continued to exert pressure on corporations, especially in connection with some of the most egregious cases in Latin American plants. Yet the broader movement has suffered important setbacks, generating some uncertainty as to the viability of the "naming and shaming" strategy and the accountability politics that underlies it. To be sure, there have been remarkable instances in which transnational solidarity networks have made significant improvements in the working lives of apparel workers in other countries, establishing new forms of transnational solidarity that are highly admirable. Such has been the case in a celebrated instance involving the Kukdong plant in Mexico (see Esbenshade 2004: 203–4; Rodriguez-Garavito 2005; Seidman 2007). Kukdong is a Korean contractor that supplies footwear for Nike and Reebok. Its workers faced corrupt and physically abusive managers who engaged in summary dismissals of insubordinate workers. Forced eventually to strike, the workers were beaten by police; dozens of their leaders were arrested, harassed, and blacklisted. Although there seemed little possibility of a remedy, several solidarity groups (especially USAS and WRC) established strong and enduring ties with the Kukdong workers. After nine months of ongoing advocacy and cross-border organizing, activists and workers made unprecedented gains. Fired workers were rehired; the plant agreed to independent monitoring; and the workers won a contract with the manufacturer. This was the first instance in which Mexican workers in the garment industry won the right to independent union representation.

Other, more far-ranging, gains have also been registered. There is now a sense of greater awareness of corporate social responsibility on the part of apparel retailers, in particular; indeed, many large retailers maintain their own monitoring staffs, with substantial budgets and the claim of autonomy. Some firms (Nike, Reebok) have now established strong reputations for their ethical commitment and conduct. Yet there is also real reason for caution regarding the consequences of the anti-sweatshop movement. For one thing, some celebrated cases of transnational activism have had decidedly mixed or even negative results. Though there is disagreement about the particulars, the movement to eliminate child labor in the Bangladesh hand-woven carpet industry eventually led to a system of product certification and labeling that in the end made few significant changes in working conditions (Seidman 2007). Indeed, as Rutgers labor scholar Ethel Brooks contends (2007), the effort to ban imports using child labor led to the firing of 10,000 children within two weeks. It was only when women and children workers mobilized on their own behalf that schools, stipends, and other supports were forthcoming for displaced child laborers. In one case, involving the retailer GUESS?, the firm actually used a proprietary system of factory monitoring as a wedge against a unionization drive in one of its own plants. (The firm took out full-page newspaper ads bearing the "No Sweat" declaration, in an effort to refute the workers' claims of abusive treatment.) Weighing much of this evidence, Brooks warns that adoption of factory codes and monitoring can easily be transformed into vehicles through which retailers can burnish their corporate brands, without making meaningful changes in the conditions of production they foster in their contractors' plants.

But much has been learned from this movement. Some of the factors that limit the success of transnational solidarity work have been brought to light. Some of these are organizational, and related to the concrete practices that codes of conduct and monitoring have thus far employed. It has become clear that the independence of the monitoring system is crucial, for example, as is the need for corporations to absorb the cost of monitoring and of the reforms needed to comply with acceptable codes of conduct. This latter point bears emphasis in the light of studies reporting that retailers often externalize monitoring and other costs on their contractors. This approach asks global suppliers to adopt costly reforms even as markets compel them to cut their costs to the bone. Lacking cost sharing, nominal improvements in working hours are often accompanied by a substantial intensification of labor in the affected plants (Yu 2007; Locke et al. 2007).

Other lessons are much broader, and reach into the structural and political nature of transnational activism itself. Several interrelated issues converge at this point. First, because activists are compelled to generate public sympathy and support for workers whose rights have been violated, they tend to focus on the most egregious instances of child labor or bodily harm, rather than the more mundane or prosaic forms of oppression workers actually face. The result is that campaigns can acquire a paternalistic cast in which the goal is framed in terms of "the protection of innocent, vulnerable victims" (Seidman 2007: 32–3). Such campaigns make it impossible to place workers in anything other than a victimized, passive role. A second issue concerns the content of transnational solidarity campaigns, which often focus primarily on "protective" rights (that is, the elimination of child labor, or the provision of a minimum wage). Important though these are, they are emphasized at the expense of other "enabling" rights (such as the freedom of association and independent unionism; see Rodriguez-Garavito 2005). The result is that international human rights campaigns "tend to avoid issues of empowerment" (Seidman 2007: 34). Yet the question of empowerment, of enabling rights, is absolutely crucial if workplace gains are to be sustainable and if factory codes are to be defined and implemented in an effective way.

Perhaps the most important lesson that has emerged from transnational activism, however, is the need for much stronger ties between activist organizations in the developed world and rank-and-file workers in the affected plants. What has been missing in much solidarity work, activists now acknowledge, are structural provisions that empower workers at the point of production, and that equip them to defend the formal rights established through factory codes of conduct. Absent such recognition, the agitation for codes and monitoring winds up as a naive exercise redolent of a neo-colonial relationship, in which transnational activists and NGOs negotiate with manufacturers and retailers entirely over the heads of the workers involved. At their best – as in the Kukdong plant in Mexico – workers are fully included in negotiations, enduring cross-border ties are established, and an emphasis is placed on workers' "enabling" rights, or on the need for structures that support workers' ability to struggle on their own behalf. It is with this broad shift in mind that Rodriguez-Garavito (2005) has proposed an "Empowered Participatory Labor Regime" (EPLR) as a model for effective transnational solidarity work. Similar calls have also been advanced by scholars such as Gay Seidman. Indeed, her *Beyond the Boycott* (2007) is in many ways a probing, careful analysis that points the way toward a second stage in this movement, reflecting the broad maturation of transnational labor activism as a whole.

Conclusion

Much of the debate over the globalization of work has tended to reflect the divisions between the advanced capitalist and the developing world. In the affluent nations, the rhetoric has centered on the protection of workers' jobs, while the discourse in the less-developed world has fastened on the question of human rights. Increasingly, however, this bifurcation is beginning to break down. Transnational activist networks that seek to defend human rights have increasingly formed common cause with labor organizations, forging links that cut across national borders, providing one important indication of this convergence. Additionally, the increasing tendency for human rights conventions is to turn their attention to the advanced capitalist democracies (as when Human Rights Watch found that United States employment relations routinely violate international conventions regarding workers' rights). This blurring of rhetorical lines is likely only to grow in the coming years, not least because the core issues that confront workers in the advanced and developing nations have increasingly converged as well, underscoring the human cost of neo-liberal policy.

At the time of writing, there is little sign that neo-liberalism has begun to lose its grip on economic and political institutions. Yet, viewed from a broader perspective, it would seem that the vision of a society regulated only by market forces offers little more than a mirage. For one thing, the economies that are growing most rapidly (most obviously that of China, but also Russia, India, and Brazil) are precisely those that accord a substantial role to state policy. Perhaps more importantly, though, are the multiple sources of instability (some would say vandalism) that neo-liberalism imposes on the societies it grips.

Ulrich Beck (2000) and Richard Sennett (1998) have both lamented the legitimacy deficit that neo-liberal capitalism creates, and which denies worker-citizens the capacity to fashion meaningful narratives with which to anchor their lives over time. Yet precisely for this reason – the weakening of communal ties in an era of neo-liberalism – Bauman (2000) detects an almost unlimited appetite for what he calls "explosive communities," which give rise to a fervent nationalism, to anti-immigrant sentiment, and to xenophobic distrust in much of the advanced capitalist world. Perhaps this is inevitable. The political effect of globalization is often to foster a widespread sense of powerlessness, inducing many in the developed world to embrace a new tribalism, as evident in the growth of parochial affiliations based on nationality, ethnicity, religion, and racial identity. In all likelihood, such convulsions cannot last; like a feverish condition, these symptoms will pass, and the other, more humane, side of globalization – its expansion of the capacity for human understanding across national boundaries – can begin to make itself felt.

7
Conclusion

This book has fastened on three fundamental questions that impinge on the nature of the work that people do. First, how has the structure of work – its vertical architecture – evolved in the contemporary era? Second, to what extent have managerial and legal interventions begun to lead work and employment opportunity beyond the gendered and racialized features that arose during earlier periods of capitalist development? And, third, how has the globalization of work impinged on the rights that workers can take for granted in the contemporary world? Although uncertainty and ambiguity surround theory and research on each of these questions, the foregoing discussion does make it possible to extract a number of final observations.

Studies premised on labor-process theory or on institutionalist approaches would seem to have pursued sharply divergent paths. The former begins with the presumption that wage labor is an inherently coercive relationship; the latter sees economic coercion as an historical feature that is destined to decline, as bureaucratic hierarchies yield center-stage to less centralized (and more collaborative) forms of work. Yet, in many respects, these perspectives have described much the same phenomena: the withering away of Fordism and the rise of more flexible (and more precarious) forms of employment. The question is how the post-Fordist regimes can best be understood.

It would, of course, be foolish to believe that the era of large, centralized work organizations – Fordism – has been relegated to the past. Capital remains highly concentrated – perhaps even more so than in the past, as Harrison has argued (1994). New technologies have enabled corporations to extend their control over ever more distant production processes (as in the logistics revolution). And the asymmetrical nature of the wage-labor relationship has if anything grown in proportion to the globalization of work. Yet the *nature* of workplace hierarchy and managerial authority has indeed evolved along novel paths. Human resources and institutional theorists have essentially euphemized these trends, airbrushing the features of the new regime with the rubric of "flexibility." Thus waves of commentators have celebrated what from their point of view constitutes the emancipation of the worker from a century of bureaucratic paternalism, and from the culture of dependency that Fordism seemed to entail. Hence the various notions of "free-agent nation" and the "boundaryless career" that have done a brisk business. Much like the concept of "progress" in the nineteenth century, the notion of "flexibility" is a highly charged, value-laden construct that is difficult to oppose.

It is easy enough to point out the hidden underside appended to flexible managerial regimes: the precarity and labor-market vulnerability they impose on workers, which multiply the elements of fear and uncertainty that attach to the employment of a growing proportion of the labor force. But the question is how workers might frame a viable response. Can the presumption of permanent employment simply be restored? Should the goal be the restoration of Fordism, or something else? And how can workers be protected against the rampant uncertainties of market volatility? There are multiple answers emerging in the literature, many of which build on imaginative efforts to provide precisely those collective supports that an increasingly individualized labor market will need to embrace (the Danish conception of "flexicurity," the German conception of work-sharing in lieu of unemployment insurance, etc.). Such efforts draw attention to a vital point that has not been given the attention it deserves: the new regimes are by their very nature politically under-determined, and thus more malleable than analysts have allowed. Their most coercive features – the casualization of work and the multiplication of uncertainty described in chapters 2 and 3 – reflect the surge of neo-liberal policies that has engulfed the advanced capitalist world, rather than the inherent features of the new regimes themselves. The vision of the institutionalists is far from mere illusion, in other words. The flexible, collaborative, and quasi-artisanal workplace they advocate may eventually provide a viable ideal – but its realization will require collectively mandated structures that provide income supports, access to real training and education, social insurance systems, and employment subsidies targeted to emerging fields, rather than the radically individualized labor market that neo-liberal policies have imposed.

This point has broader implications, reaching into the importance of political structures for the nature of the employment relationship. As just noted, the precarious quality of the post-Fordist economy stems in large part from the state-led policies that have de-regulated industries, dismantled the welfare state, encouraged the growth of financial conceptions of work, and eviscerated labor law. To a much greater extent than theorists acknowledge, the abandonment of vertically integrated structures in favor of more flexible networks and webs of capital accumulation has been politically induced. To account for the evolution of managerial regimes, and to formulate viable future paths, will require analysts of work to adopt a broader approach, bringing into our discussion the role inevitably played by political structures, which determined (however implicitly) the contours of work and employment. This point – implied in such works as Charles Sabel's *Work and Politics* (1982) and Michael Burawoy's *The Politics of Production* (1985) – requires greater attention than it has received.

Politics is obviously important, too, when we turn our attention to ascribed inequalities – to gender and racial disparities in the distribution of jobs and the rewards they can provide. Social movements supporting egalitarian policies left their mark on the workplace largely by winning legislative victories, and by reframing normative perceptions that define acceptable corporate behavior. Also, judicial rulings have powerfully shaped organizational practices, though often in ways which have tended to legitimate demographic inequalities. The missing elements concern any well-developed understanding of how legal imperatives and judicial rulings are translated into practices that directly impinge on social life at the point of production itself. Equally important is the need for studies showing how workplace culture operates to limit the opportunities that women and minorities enjoy.

As in much social theory generally, analysis of the workplace has manifested something of a "cultural turn." As the foregoing chapters have shown, normative constructs at work have seemed to play an increasingly central role in management's effort to control the labor process. As the service and hospitality industries have grown, organizations have staked out increasing claims to facets of interaction and the presentation of self that had previously stood at one remove from commercial demands. Yet our understanding of workplace culture and our ability to connect it to ascriptive inequalities have languished in an under-developed state.

One view has approached workplace culture through the lens of managerial hegemony, as if it constituted a monolithic extension of managerial goals (as in the work of Paul du Gay and James Barker, discussed above). Others instead view workplace culture as at least partly autonomous from managerial initiatives, and as sometimes adopting forms that management finds difficult or impossible to control – an approach the present author has found useful (Vallas 2003c, 2006), as has the British sociologist John Weeks. In much of the literature on pay disparities by gender and race, researchers have implied the existence of a cultural effect – a collectively defined bias that is brought to bear on the value of labor performed in segregated occupational contexts. Lacking in much of this literature is any effort to explain how such biases are formed, how they are connected to the allocation of job rewards, and whether the under-valuation of female and minority labor might stem from the greater *power* of the dominant group within the firm, or from the greater *vulnerability* of historically excluded groups. Perhaps, in the end, the linkage between cultural biases and organizational power will prove central to empirical research. Clearly, informal social relations at work have subtle yet powerful effects on the allocation of job rewards, far beyond what judicial rulings acknowledge. A clearer understanding of this fact will surely equip us to gain greater purchase on the adjudication of the gender and racial disparities that have continued to exist throughout the occupational structure.

At the most general level stands a question that is urgently advanced by the current state of global capitalism itself. As capitalism seeks to shed its Fordist trappings, propertied classes and political elites have set about uprooting virtually all collective obstacles that stand in the way of their free-market utopia (including a wide array of government regulations, trade unions, bureaucratic constraints, and much of the welfare state). Yet by insisting on projecting neo-liberalism onto the global landscape, thus opening up endless investments for capital abroad, decision-makers have introduced such instability into the global economy as to disrupt the system's operations, staining their legitimacy in ways that are difficult to control. Perhaps most important here has been the effect of these trends on the prevailing conception of work itself.

Ulrich Beck (2000) has predicted the end of the "work society" itself. In its youth, capitalism built on the Protestant Reformation, and in so doing invested work with the seemingly endless capacity for self-realization. Where the ancient Greeks had defined themselves through their rejection of mindless toil, industrial capitalism now inverted this conception, elevating work to a higher plane, thus encouraging workers to demonstrate their value precisely by engaging in work:

> The extent to which work is part of the modern European's moral being and self-image is evident from the fact that, in Western culture, it has long been the only relevant source and the only valid measure for the evaluation of human beings and their activities. Only those things which are proven and recognized to be work count as valuable. (Beck 2000: 10)

In Beck's analysis, it is precisely this normative apparatus that has come to an end. For the logical culmination of the work society is precisely a dramatic and relentless decline in the proportion of the potentially active labor force that is engaged in full-time employment, generating a "capitalism without work."

Beck is not the first to speak of a jobless recovery; nor is his the only voice raised against the "end" of work as previously defined – similar arguments have been advanced by Aronowitz and DiFazio (1995), Rifkin (2004), and Block (1990). Yet the specter of chronic labor surpluses across so much of the advanced capitalist landscape lends urgency to his diagnosis of our time. What is the future of a society that has been premised on the urge to produce – that is, on the compulsion to establish one's moral value through full-time work – when the introduction of new technologies and the global dispersion of production worldwide have eroded the very institutional platform on which the work society has historically stood?

It may be that visions of a chronic collapse of capitalism's capacity to generate full-time employment grossly over-reach their mark. Yet, even if global capitalism regains its footing, many of the cultural binaries from which it drew its strength seem to have lost their resonance. How can the idle poor be stigmatized when their ranks have begun to encompass tens of millions of people who are unable to find work in any form? Is it possible to maintain the division between paid employment and non-market work, whether performed at home or in the community, when paid, full-time employment encompasses a smaller and smaller proportion of the labor force?

Beck himself advocates institutions that might foster the growth of "civil labour" (the provision of socially useful work outside the market context) in the "multi-activity society." Abandoning the notion of rigid careers in the private market alone, his approach foresees a more fluid pattern that entails mobility across economic sectors, as workers move between types of "post-market" labor that advance one or another social need – for example, care work, or public tasks, or cultural work – even within the space of the same working week. A vital point is the need to transcend the "value imperialism" (as Beck terms it) imposed by industrial capitalism, which devalued work in its non-market form. Such approaches have nothing in common with "workfare," it should be noted.

Though programs such as this seem utopian, we are beginning to hear complaints from the most conservative policy foundations concerning the irrationality of unemployment insurance systems that only ever reward workers for the non-performance of work in any form. Policy prescriptions regarding social insurance oscillate wildly, too, from one electoral cycle to the next. In the end, the question is whether generations of exposure to neo-liberal ideology, coupled with the radically individualistic pattern that has been inscribed within both civil society and the labor market, will abort the arrival of such new conceptions of labor as this. Much hangs in the balance. There is a great deal of work to be done.

Notes

Chapter 1 Introduction

1 The British sociologist Kevin Bales (1999) has written on the persistence of unfree labor (and especially slavery) in Thailand, Pakistan, Mauritania, Brazil, India, and other societies as well. Periodic reports appear in the media regarding unfree labor in our own society, even outside of prisons. On the resurgence of sweatshops, which reflects a fusion of market and unfree labor, see Bonacich and Appelbaum (2000); Collins (2003).

2 One additional perspective broached in chapter 2 stems from the Foucauldian conception of governmentality. Examples of this approach can be found in the work of Rose (1990), du Gay (1996), and Ngai (2005).

3 In fact, feminist sociologists have often challenged Marxism, charging that it has neglected the way in which the division between mental and manual labor is itself infused with gendered meanings. Ethnographic work described further below finds that working men frequently imbue manual work with masculine bravado. Their oppositional consciousness often operates by equating office work with feminine traits (as when they challenge the manliness of the managers and engineers who oversee them). See Willis (1977) and Cockburn (1983).

4 This is one reason why the economist Heidi Hartmann founded the Institute for Women's Policy Research, a Washington, DC, think tank that compiles policy-oriented research on the obstacles that women confront within economic institutions. See: <www.iwpr.org>.

Chapter 2 Capitalism, Taylorism, and the Problem of Labor Control

1 The scientific management movement was led by Frederick W. Taylor (1856–1915), a Philadelphia-born engineer who championed efforts to nationalize industrial production processes. Taylor advocated the application of experimental methods (including, time and motion study) to determine the "one best way" of accomplishing every task. The subtext of scientific management was the effort to reduce the employer's reliance on the workmen's skill. For discussion, see Montgomery 1979, and Stark 1980.

Chapter 3 From Fordism to Flexibility?

1 Christopherson and Storper (1989) are careful to note the threats this transformation has posed to some production workers in the industry, as access to employment and rising levels of wage inequality have accompanied the rise of the flexible regime of movie-making. This whole matter of job insecurity or "precarity" is taken up further below.
2 Marcello Tarì and Ilaria Vanni (2005), "On the Life and Deeds of San Precario, Patron Saint of Precarious Workers and Lives," *Fibreculture: Internet Theory, Criticism, Research* 5: <http://journal.fibreculture.org/issue5/vanni_tari.html>. Accessed June 27, 2010. See also: <http://www.sanprecario.info/>.

Chapter 4 Ascriptive Inequalities at Work, I: Gender

1 Parallel developments occurred in Great Britain (Seccombe 1986; Humphries 1977), though apparently not in France (Frader 1996). Much more research is needed on the movements that gave rise to the male breadwinner norm, both in the United States and in other parts of the world.
2 In one landmark case alleging pay discrimination, *AFSCME v. Washington*, Judge (later Justice) Anthony Kennedy ruled against the plaintiffs, writing that "Neither law nor logic deems the free market a suspect enterprise." See Nelson and Bridges (1999).

Chapter 5 Ascriptive Inequalities, II: Race, Ethnicity, and Diversity at Work

1 A substantial literature shows that pay disparities between white and black men have persisted in spite of the convergence in levels of education that has occurred in recent years (Smith 1997, 2001). Yet more focused studies that use data on cognitive skills do find persisting skills disparities, often owing to higher rates of poverty and racial segregation in neighborhoods and consequently schools (Farkas et al. 1997).

Chapter 6 The Globalization of Work

1 One commonly used measure of globalization is trade openness (that is, the value of all imports and exports as a proportion of a nation's total economic activity). Using this measure, we find that the world economy grew increasingly global during the late twentieth century: trade openness roughly doubled from 1960 to 2003, with an apparent surge of cross-border activity during the 1990s. See Brady, Beckfield, and Zhao 2007: 314; Guillen 2001).

2 For analysis and debates concerning global commodity chains, see Gereffi (1994) and Schrank (2004).

References

Abbott, Andrew. 1988. *The System of Professions: An Essay on the Division of Expert Labor.* Chicago, IL: University of Chicago Press.

Althusser, Louis. 1971. "Ideology and Ideological State Apparatuses (Notes Toward an Investigation)," in *Lenin and Philosophy.* New York: Monthly Review, pp. 85–127.

American Federation of State, County, and Municipal Employees, *AFL-CIO (AFSCME) v. State of Washington. 1985. 770 F.2d 1401, vol. 84–3569, 84–3590,* edited by N. C. United States Court of Appeals. September 4.

Ancona, Deborah G., and Caldwell, David F. 1992. "Demography and Design: Predictors of New Product Team Performance," *Organization Science* 3/3(August): 321–41.

Appelbaum, Richard P. 2009. "Big Suppliers in Greater China: A Growing Counterweight to the Power of Giant Retailers," in H. Hung, ed., *China and the Transformation of Global Capitalism* (Themes in Global Social Change). Baltimore, MD: Johns Hopkins University Press, pp. 65–85.

Aronowitz, Stanley. 1973. *False Promises: The Shaping of American Working Class Consciousness.* New York: McGraw-Hill.

Aronowitz, Stanley, and William DiFazio. 1995. *The Jobless Future: Sci-Tech and the Dogma of Work.* Minneapolis, MN: University of Minnesota Press.

Arthur, Michael B., and Denise Rousseau. 2001. *The Boundaryless Career: A New Employment Principle for a New Organizational Era.* Oxford: Oxford University Press.

Atkinson, John. 1985. "The Changing Corporation," in D. Clutterbuck, ed., *New Patterns of Work.* London: Gower, pp. 13–34.

Avent-Holt, Dustin, and Donald Tomaskovic-Devey. 2010. "The Relational Basis of Inequality: Generic and Contingent Wage Distribution Processes," *Work and Occupations* 37: 162–19.

Avey, James B., Bradley J. West, and Craig D. Crossley. 2008. "The Association Between Ethnic Congruence in the Supervisor–Subordinate Dyad and Subordinate Organizational Position and Salary," *Journal of Occupational and Organizational Psychology* 81/3: 55–66.

Bair, Jennifer. 2005. "Global Capitalism and Commodity Chains: Looking Back, Going Forward," *Competition and Change* 9/2 (June): 153–80.

Baldi, Stephanie, and Debra B. McBrier. 1997. "Do the Determinants of Promotion Differ for Blacks and Whites?," *Work and Occupations* 24 (November): 478–97.

Bales, Kevin. 1999. *Disposable People: New Slavery in the Global Economy*. Berkeley, CA: University of California Press.

Barboza, David. 2010. "Clues in an iPhone Autopsy," in *New York Times*, 6 July: B1. Available at: <http://www.nytimes.com/2010/07/06/technology/06iphone.html?n=Top%2fReference%2fTimes%20Topics%2fSubjects%2fT%2fTelephones%20and%20Telecommunications>.

Barker, James R. 1993. "Tightening the Iron Cage: Concertive Control in Self-Managing Teams," *Administrative Science Quarterly* 38/3 (September): 408–37.

Barley, Steve. 2010. "Building an Institutional Field to Corral a Government: A Case to Set an Agenda for Organization Studies," *Organization Studies* 31/6 (June): 777–805.

Barley, Stephen R., and Gideon Kunda. 1992. "Design and Devotion: Surges of Rational and Normative Ideologies of Managerial Control," *Administrative Science Quarterly* 37/3: 363–99.

Bartley, Tim, and Curtis Child. 2007. "Shaming the Corporation: Reputation, Globalization, and the Dynamics of Anti-Corporate Movements." Bloomington, IN: Department of Sociology, Indiana University, unpublished ms.

Bauman, Zygmunt. 2000. *Liquid Modernity*. Cambridge: Polity.

Baxter, Janeen, and Erik Olin Wright. 2000. "The Glass Ceiling Hypothesis: A Comparative Study of the United States, Sweden, and Australia," *Gender & Society* 14/2 (April): 275–94.

Bearman, Peter. 2005. *Doormen*. Chicago, IL: University of Chicago Press.

Beck, Ulrich. 2000. *The Brave New World of Work*. Cambridge: Polity.

Becker, Gary S. [1964] 1993. *Human Capital: A Theoretical and Empirical Analysis, with Special Reference to Education*, 3rd edn. Chicago, IL: University of Chicago Press.

Becker, Howard Saul. 1963. *Outsiders: Studies in the Sociology of Deviance.* London: Free Press of Glencoe.

Bell, Daniel. 1973. *The Coming of Post-Industrial Society.* New York: Basic Books.

Bennhold, Katrin. 2006. "Failure of Jobs Law May Halt New Bids for French Labor Reform," in *New York Times*, April 11. Available at: <http://www.nytimes.com/2006/04/11/world/europe/11iht-france. html?ref=katrinbennhold>.

Bensman, Joseph, and Robert Lilienfeld. 1991. *Craft and Consciousness: Occupational Technique and the Development of World Images.* New York: Aldine de Gruyter.

Berggren, Christian. 1992. *Alternatives to Lean Production: Work Organization in the Swedish Auto Industry.* Ithaca, NY: ILR Press.

Bernhardt, Annette, Heather Boushey, Laura Dresser, and Chris Tilly, eds. 2008. "Introduction to the 'Gloves-Off' Economy," in *The Gloves-Off Economy: Workplace Standards at the Bottom of America's Labor Market.* University of Illinois, Champaign: Labor and Employment Relations Association, pp. 1–30.

Bertrand, Marianne, and Sendhil Mullainathan. 2004. "Are Emily and Greg More Employable Than Lakisha and Jamal? A Field Experiment on Labor Market Discrimination," *American Economic Review* 94/4: 991–1013.

Bettie, Julie. 2003. *Women without Class: Girls, Race, and Identity.* Berkeley, CA: University of California Press.

Bhagwati, Jagdish N. 2004. *In Defense of Globalization.* New York: Oxford University Press.

Blair-Loy, M. 2001. "It's Not Just What You Know, It's Who You Know: Technical Knowledge, Rainmaking, and Gender among Finance Executives," *Research in the Sociology of Work* 10/51: 83.

Blalock, Hubert M. 1967. *Toward a Theory of Minority-Group Relations.* New York: Wiley.

Blinder, Alan S. 2006. "Offshoring: The Next Industrial Revolution?," *Foreign Affairs* 85/2 (March/April): 113–28.

Block, Fred L. 1990. *Postindustrial Possibilities: A Critique of Economic Discourse.* Berkeley, CA: University of California Press.

Blumer, Herbert. 1958. "Race Prejudice as a Sense of Group Position," *Pacific Sociological Review* 1 (spring): 3–7.

Bockman, Johanna, and Michael Bernstein. 2008. "Scientific Community in a Divided World: Economists, Planning, and Research Priority during the Cold War," *Comparative Studies in Society and History* 50 (July): 581–613.

Bodnar, Chris. 2006. "Taking it to the Streets: French Cultural Worker Resistance and the Creation of a Precariat Movement," *Canadian Journal of Communication* 31/3: 675–94.

Bolton, S. C., and Boyd, C. 2003. "Trolley Dolly or Skilled Emotion Manager? Moving on from Hochschild's Managed Heart," *Work, Employment and Society* 17: 289–308.

Bonacich, Edna, and Richard P. Appelbaum. 2000. *Behind the Label: Inequality in the Los Angeles Apparel Industry.* Berkeley, CA: University of California Press.

Bonacich, Edna, and Jake B. Wilson. 2008. *Getting the Goods: Ports, Labor, and the Logistics Revolution.* Ithaca, NY: Cornell University Press.

Bourdieu, Pierre. 1984. *Distinction: A Social Critique of the Judgment of Taste.* Cambridge, MA: Harvard University Press.

Boyenge, J. P. S. 2007. *ILO Database on Export Processing Zones* (revised). Geneva: International Labour Office.

Braddock, J. H. II, and McPartland, James M. 1987. "How Minorities Continue to be Excluded from Equal Employment Opportunities: Research on Labor Market and Institutional Barriers," *Journal of Social Issues* 43/1 (spring): 5–39.

Brady, David, Jason Beckfield, and Wei Zhao. 2007. "The Consequences of Economic Globalization for Affluent Democracies," *Annual Review of Sociology* 33 (August): 313–34.

Braverman, Harry. 1974. *Labor and Monopoly Capital.* New York: Monthly Review.

Brody, David. 1980. *Workers in Industrial America: Essays on the Twentieth Century Struggle.* New York: Oxford University Press.

Bronfenbrenner, K. 2000. *Uneasy Terrain: The Impact of Capital Mobility on Workers, Wages, and Union Organizing.* Ithaca, NY: Cornell University School of Industrial and Labor Relations.

Bronfenbrenner, K., and Luce, S. 2004. *The Changing Nature of Corporate Global Restructuring: The Impact of Production Shifts on Jobs in the US, China, and around the Globe.* Washington, DC: US–China Economic and Security Review Commission.

Brooks, Ethel Carolyn. 2007. *Unraveling the Garment Industry: Transnational Organizing and Women's Work.* Minneapolis, MN: University of Minnesota Press.

Browne, Irene, and Joya Misra. 2003. "The Intersection of Gender and Race in Labor Markets," *Annual Review of Sociology* 29: 27.

Brubaker, Rogers. November 1985. "Rethinking Classical Theory: The Sociological Vision of Pierre Bourdieu," *Theory and Society* 14/6: (November): 745–75.

Brusco, S. 1982. "The Emilian Model: Productive Decentralisation and Social Integration," *Cambridge Journal of Economics* 6: 18.

Burawoy, Michael. 1979. *Manufacturing Consent: Changes in the Labor Process Under Monopoly Capitalism.* Chicago, IL: University of Chicago Press.

Burawoy, Michael. 1985. *The Politics of Production: Factory Regimes Under Capitalism and Socialism*. London: Verso.

Bureau, US Census. 2009, "Population Finder," *American Fact Finder: Population Finder*, at: <http://factfinder.census.gov/servlet/SAFFPopulation>.

Cainelli, Giulio, and Nicola de Liso. 2005. "Innovation in Industrial Districts: Evidence from Italy," *Industry and Innovation* 12: 383–98.

Cambois, E. 2004. "Careers and Mortality: Evidences on How Far Occupational Mobility Predicts Differentiated Risks," *Social Science and Medicine* 58: 2545–58.

Casey, Catherine. 1995. *Work, Self, and Society: After Industrialism*. London: Sage.

Castells, Manuel. 1996. *The Rise of the Network Society*. Malden, MA: Blackwell.

Castilla, Emilio J. 2008. "Gender, Race, and Meritocracy in Organizational Careers," *American Journal of Sociology* 113/6: 1479–1526.

Castilla, Emilio J., and Stephen Benard. 2010. "The Paradox of Meritocracy in Organizations," *Administrative Science Quarterly* 55/4: 543–76.

Catanzarite, Lisa. 2003. "Race-Gender Composition and Occupational Pay Degradation," *Social Problems* 50–1 (February): 14–37.

Charles, Maria, and David B. Grusky. 2004. *Occupational Ghettoes: The Worldwide Segregation of Women*. Stanford, CA: Stanford University Press.

Chen, Liang-Chih. 2009. "Learning through Informal Local and Global Linkages: The Case of Taiwan's Machine Tool Industry," *Research Policy* 38/3: 527–35.

Christopherson, Susan, and Michael Storper. 1989. "The Effects of Flexible Specialization on Industrial Politics and the Labor Market: The Motion Picture Industry," *Industrial & Labor Relations Review* 42/3 (April): 331–47.

Cockburn, Cynthia. 1983. *Brothers: Male Dominance and Technological Change*. London: Pluto Press.

Cohen, Philip N., and Matt L. Huffman. 2003. "Occupational Segregation and the Devaluation of Women's Work across U.S. Labor Markets," *Social Forces* 81/3 (March): 881–908.

Cohen, Philip N., Matt L. Huffman, and S. Knauer. 2009. "Stalled Progress? Gender Segregation and Wage Inequality among Managers, 1980–2000," *Work and Occupations* 36: 318–42.

Cohn, Samuel. 1985. *The Process of Occupational Sex-typing: The Feminization of Clerical Labor in Great Britain*. Philadelphia, PA: Temple University Press.

Collins, J. L. 2003. *Threads: Gender, Labor, and Power in the Global Apparel Industry.* Chicago, IL: University of Chicago Press.

Collins, J. L. 2005. "New Directions in Commodity Chain Analysis of Global Development Processes," in Frederick H. Buttel and Philip McMichael, eds, *New Directions in the Sociology of Global Development (Research in Rural Sociology and Development, Volume 11),* Bradford, Yorkshire: Emerald Group Publishing Limited, pp. 3–17.

Collins, Patricia Hill. 2000. *Black Feminist Thought: Knowledge, Consciousness, and the Politics of Empowerment.* New York: Routledge.

Collins, Sharon. 1997. *Black Corporate Employees: The Making and Breaking of a Black Middle Class.* Philadelphia, PA: Temple University Press.

Congressional Budget Office. December 23, 2008. *Factors Underlying the Decline in Manufacturing Employment Since 2000.* Washington DC; available at: <http://www.cbo.gov/doc.cfm?index=9749>.

Cotter, David A., Joan M. Hermsen, and Reeve Vanneman. 2004. *Gender Inequality at Work.* New York: Russell Sage Foundation and Population Reference Bureau.

Cotter, David A., J. M. Hermsen, S. Ovadia, and Reeve Vanneman. 2001. "The Glass Ceiling Effect," *Social Forces* 80/2: 655–81.

Cox, Oliver Cromwell. 1948. *Caste, Class, & Race: A Study in Social Dynamics.* Garden City, New York: Doubleday.

Crenshaw, Kimberle. 1991. "Mapping the Margins: Intersectionality, Identity Politics, and Violence Against Women of Color," *Stanford Law Review* 43: 1241–99.

Cushman, John H., Jr. 1998. "Nike Pledges to End Child Labor and Increase Safety," in *New York Times*, May 13. Available at: <http://www.nytimes.com/1998/05/13/business/international-business-nike-pledges-to-end-child-labor-and-apply-us-rules-abroad.html?scp=1&sq=Cushman,%20John%20H.,%20Jr.%20+%20Nike&st=cse>.

de Grazia, Sebastian. 1994. *Of Time, Work and Leisure.* New York: Vintage.

DiMaggio, Paul, and Walter W. Powell. 1983. "The Iron Cage Revisited: Institutional Isomorphism and Collective Rationality in Organizational Fields," *American Sociological Review* 48: 147–60.

DiMaggio, Paul, and Walter W. Powell, eds. 1991. "Introduction," *The New Institutionalism in Organizational Analysis.* Chicago, IL: University of Chicago Press, pp. 1–40.

Dobbin, Frank. 1994. *Forging Industrial Policy: The United States, Britain, and France in the Railway Age.* Cambridge: Cambridge University Press.

Dobbin, Frank 2009. *Inventing Equal Opportunity*. Princeton, NJ: Princeton University Press.

Dobbs, Lou. 2004. *Exporting America: Why Corporate Greed is Shipping American Jobs Overseas*. New York: Warner Books.

Dohse, K., U. Jürgens, and T. Malsch. 1985. "From 'Fordism' to 'Toyotism'? The Social Organization of the Labor Process in the Japanese Automobile Industry," *Politics and Society* 14: 115–46.

Dorgan, Byron L. 2006. *Take This Job and Ship It: How Corporate Greed and Brain–Dead Politics Are Selling Out America*. New York: Thomas Dunne Books/St Martin's Press.

Dowd Hall, Jacqueline. 2000. *Like a Family: The Making of a Southern Cotton Mill World*. Chapel Hill, NC: University of North Carolina Press.

du Gay, Paul. 1996. *Consumption and Identity at Work*. Thousand Oaks, CA: Sage.

du Gay, P., and G. Salaman. 1992. "The Cult(ure) of the Customer," *Journal of Management Studies* 29/5: 615–33.

Edelman, L. 1990. "Legal Environments and Organizational Governance: The Expansion of Due Process in the American Workplace," *American Journal of Sociology* 95: 1401.

Edelman, Lauren B., Sally Riggs Fuller, and Iona Mara-Drita. 2001. "Diversity Rhetoric and the Managerialization of Law," *The American Journal of Sociology* 106: 1589.

Edwards, Richard. 1979. *Contested Terrain*. New York: Basic Books.

Ehrenreich, Barbara, and Arlie Russell Hochschild. 2003. *Global Woman: Nannies, Maids, and Sex Workers in the New Economy*. New York: Metropolitan Books.

Ely, Robin J., and David A. Thomas. 2001. "Cultural Diversity at Work: The Effect of Diversity Perspectives and Diversity Processes," *Administrative Science Quarterly* 46: 229–73.

England, Paula, Paul D. Allison, and Yuxiao Wu. 2007. "Does Bad Pay Cause Occupations to Feminize, Does Feminization Reduce Pay, and How Can We Tell with Longitudinal Data?," *Social Science Research* 36: 20.

Esbenshade, Jill. 2004. *Monitoring Sweatshops: Workers, Consumers, and the Global Apparel Industry*. Philadelphia, PA: Temple University Press.

Farkas, George, Paula England, Keven Vicknair, and Barbara Kilbourne. 1997. "Cognitive Skill, Skill Demands of Jobs, and Earnings Among Young European-American, African-American, and Mexican-American Workers," *Social Forces* 75/3: 913–40.

Favreault, Melissa. 2008. *Discrimination and Economic Mobility*. Philadelphia, PA, and Washington, DC: The Pew Charitable Trusts.

Fine, Gary Alan. 1984. "Negotiated Orders and Organizational Cultures," *Annual Review of Sociology* 10: 239–62.

Fine, Gary Alan. 1996. *Kitchens: The Culture of Restaurant Work.* Berkeley, CA: University of California Press.

Fligstein, Neil. 1985. "The Spread of the Multidivisional Form, 1919–79," *American Sociological Review* 50: 15.

Fligstein, Neil. 2001. *The Architecture of Markets: An Economic Sociology of Capitalist Societies.* Princeton, NJ: Princeton University Press.

Florida, Richard L. 2003. *The Rise of the Creative Class: And How It's Transforming Work, Leisure, Community and Everyday Life.* New York: Basic Books.

Foti, A. 2004. "Precarity and N/european Identity. Interview with Merjin Oudenampsen and Gavin Sullivan," *Greenpepper Magazine.* Available at: <http://process.greenpeppermagazine.org/tiki-index. php?page= Precarity+%3A+Issue+Proposal>; accessed July 2010.

Frader, Laura. 1996. "Engendering Work and Wages: The French Labor Movement and the Family Wage," in Laura Frader and Sonya Rose, eds, *Gender and Class in Modern Europe.* Ithaca, NY: Cornell University Press, 1996, pp. 142–64.

Fraser, Jill Andresky. 2002. *White Collar Sweatshop: The Deterioration of Work and Its Rewards in Corporate America.* New York: Norton.

Gabriel, Yiannis. 2009. "Conclusion – Latte Capitalism and Late Capitalism: Reflections on Fantasy and Care as Part of the Service Triangle," in Marek Korczynski and Cameron McDonald, eds, *Service Work: Critical Perspectives.* New York: Routledge, pp. 175–91.

Gereffi, Gary. 1994. "The Organization of Buyer-Driven Global Commodity Chains: How US Retailers Shape Overseas Production Networks," in Gary Gereffi and Miguel Korzeniewicz, eds, *Commodity Chains and Global Capitalism.* Westport: Greenwood, pp. 95–122.

Gereffi, Gary. 2001. "Beyond the Producer-driven/Buyer-driven Dichotomy: The Evolution of Global Value Chains in the Internet Era," *Institute of Development Studies Bulletin* 32/3: 30–40.

Gieryn, Thomas F. 1983. "Boundary-Work and the Demarcation of Science from Non-Science: Strains and Interests in Professional Ideologies of Scientists," *American Sociological Review* (American Sociological Association) 48: 781–95.

Goffman, Erving. 1959. *The Presentation of Self in Everyday Life.* Garden City, NY: Doubleday.

Goffman, Erving. 1967. *Interaction Ritual: Essays on Face-to-Face Behavior.* Garden City, NY: Anchor Books.

Gorman, Elizabeth, and Julie Kmec, 2009. "Hierarchical Rank and Women's Organizational Mobility: Glass Ceilings in Corporate Law Firms," *American Journal of Sociology* 114/15 (March): 1428–74.

Graham, Laurie. 1995. *On the Line at Subaru-Isuzu*. Ithaca, NY: Cornell University School of Industrial and Labor Relations.

Grenier, Guillermo. 1988. *Inhuman Relations: Quality Circles and Anti-Unionism in American Industry*. Philadelphia, PA: Temple University Press.

Grugulis, Irena, Tony Dundon, and Adrian Wilkinson. 2000. "Cultural Control and the 'Culture Manager': Employment Practices in a Consultancy," *Work, Employment and Society* 14/1: 97–116.

Guillen, Mauro F. 2001. "Is Globalization Civilizing, Destructive or Feeble? A Critique of Five Key Debates in the Social-Science Literature," *Annual Review of Sociology* 27: 235–60.

Guillen, Mauro F. 1994. *Models of Management: Work, Authority and Organization in a Comparative Perspective*. Chicago, IL: University of Chicago Press.

Hakanson, Lars. 2005. "Epistemic Communities and Cluster Dynamics: On the Role of Knowledge in Industrial Districts," *Industry and Innovation* 12/4 (December): 433–63.

Halle, David. 1984. *America's Working Man: Work, Home, and Politics among Blue-Collar Property Owners*. Chicago, IL: University of Chicago Press.

Hamilton, Darrick. 2006. "The Racial Composition of American Jobs," in G. Curry, ed., *The State of Black America*. New York: The National Urban League.

Harrison, Bennett. 1994. *Lean and Mean: The Changing Landscape of Corporate Power in the Age of Flexibility*. New York: Basic Books.

Harvey, David. 1989. *The Condition of Postmodernity: An Enquiry into the Origins of Cultural Change*. Oxford: Blackwell.

Harvey, David. 2005. *A Brief History of Neo-Liberalism*. Oxford: Oxford University Press.

Heckman, James, and Peter Siegelman. 1993. "The Urban Institute Audit Studies: Their Methods and Findings," in M. Fix and R. J. Struyk, eds, *Clear and Convincing Evidence*. Washington, DC: The Urban Institute, pp. 187–258.

Hirst, Paul, and Jonathan Zeitlin. 1991. "Flexible Specialization versus Post-Fordism: Theory, Evidence and Policy Implications," *Economy and Society* 20/1 (February): 1–56.

Ho, Karen. 2009a. "Disciplining Investment Bankers, Disciplining the Economy: Wall Street's Institutional Culture of Crisis and the Downsizing of American Corporations," *American Anthropologist* 111: 177–89.

Ho, Karen Zouwen. 2009b. *Liquidated: An Ethnography of Wall Street*. Durham, NC: Duke University Press.

Hobsbawm, Eric. 1996. *The Age of Revolution 1789–1848*. New York: Vintage.

Hochschild, Arlie. 1983. *The Managed Heart: The Commercialization of Human Feeling*. Berkeley, CA: University of California Press.

Hochschild, Arlie. 2001. *The Time Bind: When Work Becomes Home and Home Becomes Work*. New York: Holt.

Hodson, Randy. 1995. "Worker Resistance: An Underdeveloped Concept in the Sociology of Work," *Economic and Industrial Democracy* 16: 79–110.

Hodson, Randy. 2001. *Dignity at Work*. New York: Cambridge University Press.

Hondagneu-Sotelo, Pierrette. 2001. *Doméstica: Immigrant Workers Cleaning and Caring in the Shadows of Affluence*. Berkeley, CA: University of California Press.

Huffman, Matt L., and Lisa Torres. 2002. "It's Not Only 'Who You Know' That Matters: Gender, Personal Contacts, and Job Lead Quality," *Gender and Society* 16/6: 793–813.

Hughes, Everett C. 1946. "The Knitting of Racial Groups in Industry," *American Sociological Review* 11/5: 512–19.

Hughes, Everett C. 1994 [1951]. "Work and Self," in L. A. Coser, ed., *On Work, Race, and the Sociological Imagination*. Chicago, IL: University of Chicago Press, pp. 57–66.

Humphries, Jane. 1977. "Class Struggle and the Persistence of the Working Class Family." *Cambridge Journal of Economics* 3: 241–58.

Hymowitz, Carol, and Timothy D. Schellhardt. 1986. "The Glass Ceiling: Why Women Can't Seem to Break the Invisible Barrier That Blocks Them from the Top Jobs," in *Wall Street Journal*, March 24: section 4, p. 1.

Ibarra, Herminia. 1995. "Race, Opportunity, and Diversity of Social Circles in Managerial Networks." *Academy of Management Journal* 38: 31.

Jacobs, Jerry A., and Kathleen Gerson. 2004. *The Time Divide: Work, Family, and Gender Inequality*. Cambridge, MA: Harvard University Press.

Jargon, Julie. August 2009. "Latest Starbucks Buzzword: 'Lean' Japanese Techniques," in *The Wall Street Journal*, August: A1. Available at: <http://online.wsj.com/article/SB124933474023402611.html?mod=djem_>.

Johnson, Spencer. 1998. *Who Moved My Cheese?: An Amazing Way to Deal with Change in Your Work and in Your Life*. New York: Putnam.

Kalev, Alexandra. 2009. "Cracking the Glass Cages? Restructuring and Ascriptive Inequality at Work," *American Journal of Sociology* 114/6: 1591–1643.

Kalev, Alexandra, Frank Dobbin, and Erin Kelly. 2006. "Best Practices or Best Guesses? Assessing the Efficacy of Corporate Affirmative

Action and Diversity Policies," *American Sociological Review* 71/4: 589–617.

Kalleberg, Arne L. 2009. "Precarious Work, Insecure Workers: Employment Relations in Transition," *American Sociological Review* 74/1 (February): 1–22.

Kalleberg, Arne L., Barbara F. Reskin, and Ken Hudson. 2000. "Bad Jobs in America: Standard and Nonstandard Employment Relations and Job Quality in the United States," *American Sociological Review* 65 (April): 256–78.

Kanter, Rosabeth Moss. 1977. *Men and Women of the Corporation.* New York: Basic Books.

Kaplinsky, Raphael. 2001. "Is Globalization All It Is Cracked Up to Be?," *Review of International Political Economy and Society* 8: 21.

Karasek R. 1979. "Job Decision Latitude, Job Demands and Mental Strain: Implications for Job Redesign," *Administrative Science Quarterly* 24: 285–308.

Karasek, R. A. 1981. "Job Socialization and Job Strain: The Implications of Two Related Psychological Mechanisms for Job Design," in B. Gardell and G. Johansson, eds, *Working Life.* New York: John Wiley & Sons, pp. 75–94.

Kasinitz, Philip, and Jan Rosenberg. 1996. "Missing the Connection: Social Isolation and Employment on the Brooklyn Waterfront," *Social Problems* 43 (May): 17.

Keck, Margaret E., and Kathryn Sikkink. 1998. *Activists Beyond Borders: Advocacy Networks in International Politics.* Ithaca, NY: Cornell University Press.

Kerber, Linda K. 1988. "Separate Spheres, Female Worlds, Woman's Place: The Rhetoric of Women's History," *The Journal of American History* 75/1: 9–39.

Kern, Horst, and Michael Schumann. 1989. "New Concepts of Production in West German Plants," in Peter Katzenstein, ed., *Industry and Politics in West Germany.* Ithaca, NY: Cornell University Press, pp. 87–112.

Kern, Horst, and Michael Schumann. 1992. "New Concepts of Production and the Emergence of the Systems Controller," in P. Adler, ed., *Technology and the Future of Work.* New York: Oxford University Press, pp. 111–48.

Kessler-Harris, Alice. 1982. *Out to Work: A History of Wage-Earning Women in the United States.* New York: Oxford University Press.

Klein, Naomi. 2000. *No Logo: Taking Aim at the Brand Bullies.* Toronto: Knopf Canada.

Kmec, Julie A. 2003. "Minority Job Concentration and Wages," *Social Problems* 50/1: 38–59.

Knight, Don, Craig L. Pearce, Ken G. Smith, and Judy D. Olian. 1999. "Top Management Team Diversity, Group Process, and Strategic Consensus," *Strategic Management Journal* 20: 445–65.

Knights, David, and Darren McCabe. 2000. "'Ain't Misbehavin?' Opportunities for Resistance under New Forms of 'Quality' Management," *Sociology* 34/3: 421–36.

Kohn, Melvin L. 1969. *Class and Conformity: A Study in Values*. Homewood, IL: Dorsey Press.

Kohn, Melvin L., and Carmi Schooler. 1983. *Work and Personality: An Inquiry in the Impact of Social Stratification*. Norwood, NJ: Ablex Publishing Corporation.

Korczynski, Marek. 2009. "Understanding the Contradictory Lived Experience of Service Work: The Customer-Oriented Bureaucracy," in Marek Korczyski and Cameron McDonald, eds. *Service Work: Critical Perspectives*. New York: Routledge, pp. 73–90.

Korczynski, Marek, and Cameron Macdonald. 2009. *Service Work: Critical Perspectives*. New York: Routledge.

Kornhauser, Arthur William. 1965. *Mental Health of the Industrial Worker: A Detroit Study*. New York: Wiley.

Krinsky, John. 2007. *Free Labor: Workfare and the Contested Language of Neoliberalism*. Chicago, IL: University of Chicago Press.

Kristof, Nicholas. 2009. "My Sweatshop Column," in *New York Times*, January 14. Available at: <http://kristof.blogs.nytimes.com/2009/01/14/my-sweatshop-column/?ref=opinion>.

Kristof, N., and S. Wu Dunn. 2000. "Two Cheers for Sweatshops," in *New York Times*, (September 24) 6 (magazine): 70–1. Available at: <http://www.nytimes.com/2000/09/24/magazine/two-cheers-for-sweatshops.html>.

Kunda, Gideon. 1992. *Engineering Culture*. Cambridge, MA: MIT Press.

Kunda, Gideon, and Galit Ailon-Souday. 2005. "Managers, Markets, and Ideologies: Design and Devotion Revisited," in *The Oxford Handbook of Work and Organization*. Oxford: Oxford University Press, pp. 200–19.

Lamont, Michele. 1992. *Money, Morals, and Manners: The Culture of the French and the American Upper-Middle Class*. Chicago, IL: University of Chicago Press.

Lash, Scott, and John Urry. 1987. *The End of Organized Capitalism*. Madison, WI: University of Wisconsin Press.

LaVaque-Manty, Mika. 2007. "American Exceptionalism, Part 42: The Case of the Missing Precariat." Paper presented at the Annual Meetings of the Western Political Science Association, Chicago.

Lee, Ching Kwan. 1998. *Gender and the South China Miracle: Two*

Worlds of Factory Women. Berkeley, CA: University of California Press.

Lee, Jennifer. 2000. "The Salience of Race in Everyday Life: Black Customers' Shopping Experiences in Black and White Neighborhoods," *Work and Occupations* 27 (August): 24.

Leidner, Robin. 1993. *Fast Food, Fast Talk*. Berkeley, CA: University of California Press.

Leidner, Rüdiger, and European Commission. Enterprise DG. Unit D.3. 2004. *The European Tourism Industry: A Multi-Sector with Dynamic Markets: Structures, Developments and Importance for Europe's Economy*. Luxembourg: Office for Official Publications of the European Communities.

Lerner, Gerda. 1969. "The Lady and the Mill Girl: Changes in the Status of Women in the Age of Jackson, 1800–1840." *American Studies Journal* 10/1: 5–15.

Levanon, Asaf, Paula England, and Paul Allison. 2009. "Occupational Feminization and Pay: Assessing Causal Dynamics Using 1950–2000 U.S. Census Data," *Social Forces* 88 (December): 865–91.

Lichtenstein, Nelson. 2006. *Wal-Mart: The Face of Twenty-First-Century Capitalism*. New York: New Press.

Lichtenstein, Richard, Jeffrey A. Alexander, Kimberly Jinnett, and Esther Ullman. 1997. "Embedded Intergroup Relations in Interdisciplinary Teams: Effects on Perceptions of Levels of Team Integration," *Journal of Applied Behavioral Science* 33/4: 413–34.

Light, Ryan, Vincent J. Roscigno, and Alexandra Kalev. 2011. "Racial Discrimination, Interpretation, and Legitimacy at Work," *Annals of the American Academy of Political and Social Science* 634: 39–59.

Linnehan, F., and Konrad, A. M. 1999. "Diluting Diversity: Implications for Inter-Group Inequality in Organizations," *Journal of Management Inquiry* 8/4: 399–414.

Littler, C., and Salaman, G. 1982. "Bravermania and Beyond – Recent Theories of the Labour Process," *Sociology* 16/2: 251–69.

Locke, Richard, Fei Qin, and Alberto Brause. 2007. "Does Monitoring Improve Labor Standards?: Lessons from Nike," *Industrial and Labor Relations Review* 61/1: 3–31.

Maanen, John Van. 1991. "The Smile Factory," in P. Frost et al., eds, *Reframing Organizational Culture*. Newbury Park, CA: Sage Publications, pp. 58–76.

McCall, Leslie. 2001. *Complex Inequality: Gender, Class, and Race in the New Economy*. New York: Routledge.

Macdonald, Cameron L., and Carmen Sirianni. 1996. "The Service Society and the Changing Experience of Work," in McDonald and Sirianni, eds, *Working in the Service Society*. Philadelphia, PA: Temple University Press, pp. 1–26.

Macdonald, Cameron L., and David Merrill. 2009. "Intersectionality in the Emotional Proletariat: A New Lens on Employment Discrimination in Service Work," in Marek Korczynski and Cameron MacDonald, eds, *Service Work: Critical Perspectives*. New York: Routledge, pp. 113–35.

McDonald, Steve, and Jacob C. Day. 2010 [2002]. "Race, Gender, and the Invisible Hand of Social Capital," *Sociology Compass* 4 (July): 12.

McDonald, Steve, Nan Lin, and Dan Ao. 2009. "Networks of Opportunity: Gender, Race and Unsolicited Job Leads," *Social Problems* 56: 18.

McIlwee, Judith Samsom, and J. Gregg Robinson. 1992. *Women in Engineering: Gender, Power, and Workplace Culture*. Albany, NY: State University of New York Press.

Marshall, Alfred. 1910. *Principles of Economics: An Introductory Volume*. London: Macmillan and Co. Limited.

Marx, Karl. 1967 [1865]. *Capital*, Volume I: New York: International.

Maume, David J. 1999. "Glass Ceilings and Glass Escalators: Occupational Segregation and Race and Sex Differences in Managerial Promotions," *Work and Occupations* 26/4: 483–509.

Maume, David J., Jr. 2004. "Is the Glass Ceiling a Unique Form of Inequality? Evidence From a Random-Effects Model of Managerial Attainment," *Work and Occupations* 31 (May): 250–74.

Meyer, J., and B. Rowan. 1977. "Institutional Organizations: Formal Structure as Myth and Ceremony," *American Journal of Sociology* 83/2: 340–63.

Meyer, J., and W. Richard Scott. 1992. *Organizational Environments: Ritual and Rationality*. Thousand Oaks, CA: Sage.

Milkman, Ruth. 1987. *Gender at Work: The Dynamics of Job Segregation by Sex During World War II*. Urbana, IL: University of Illinois Press.

Monds, Jean. 1976. "Worker's Control and the Historians: A New Economism," *New Left Review* 1 (May–June): 81–104.

Montgomery, David. 1979. *Workers' Control in America: Studies in the History of Work, Technology, and Labor Struggles*. New York: Cambridge University Press.

Montgomery, David. 1987. *The Fall of the House of Labor: The Workplace, the State, and American Labor Activism, 1865–1925*. Cambridge: Cambridge University Press.

Mosley, Layna, and Saika Uno. 2007. "Racing to the Bottom or Climbing to the Top? Economic Globalization and Labor Rights," *Comparative Political Studies* 40/ 8 (August): 923–48.

Moss, P., and Tilly, C. 1996. "Soft Skills and Race: An Investigation of Black Men's Employment Problems," *Work and Occupations* 23/3: 252–76.

Mouw, Ted. 2002. "Are Black Workers Missing the Connection? The Effect of Spatial Distance and Employee Referrals on Interfirm Racial Segregation," *Demography* 39/3: 507–28.

Neilson, B., and Rossiter, N. 2008. "Precarity as a Political Concept, or, Fordism as Exception," *Theory, Culture & Society* 25/7–8: 51–72.

Nelson, Robert L., and William P. Bridges. 1999. *Legalizing Gender Inequality: Courts, Markets, and Unequal Pay for Women in America*. Cambridge: Cambridge University Press.

Ngai, Pun. 2005. *Made in China: Women Factory Workers in a Global Workplace*. Durham, NC: Duke University Press.

Ngai,Pun, and Chris Smith. 2007. "Putting Transnational Labour Process in its Place: The Dormitory Labour Regime in Post-Socialist China," *Work, Employment and Society* 21/1: 27–45.

Nichols, Theo, Surhan Cam, Wen-chi Grace Chou, Soonok Chun, Wei Zhao, and Tongqing Feng. 2004. "Factory Regimes and the Dismantling of Established Labour in Asia: A Review of Cases from Large Manufacturing Plants in China, South Korea and Taiwan," *Work, Employment, and Society* 18: 663–84.

Nickson, D., and C. Warhurst. 2007. "Opening Pandora's Box: Aesthetic Labour and Hospitality," in Conrad Lashley, Paul Lynch, and Alison J. Morrison, eds, *Hospitality: A Social Lens*. London: Elsevier, pp. 155–71.

Nickson, D., and C. Warhurst. 2007. "Employee Experience of Aesthetic Labour in Retail and Hospitality," *Work, Employment and Society* 21/1 (March): 103–20.

Noble, David F. 1984. *Forces of Production: A Social History of Industrial Automation*. Oxford: Oxford University Press.

Ong, Aihwa. 2006. *Neoliberalism as Exception: Mutations in Citizenship and Sovereignty*. Durham, NC: Duke University Press.

Orlikowski, Wanda. 2007. "Sociomaterial Practices: Exploring Technology at Work," *Organization Studies* 28: 1435–48.

Orr, Julian E. 1996. *Talking About Machines: An Ethnography of a Modern Job*. Ithaca, NY: Cornell University School of Industrial and Labor Relations.

Osnowitz, Debra. 2011. *Freelancing Expertise: Contract Professionals in the New Economy*. Ithaca, NY: Cornell University School of Industrial and Labor Relations.

Owen-Smith, Jason and W.W. Powell. 2004. "Knowledge Networks as Channels and Conduits: The Effects of Spillovers in the Boston Biotechnology Community," *Organization Science* 15/1: 5–21.

Padavic, Irene. 2005. "Laboring Under Uncertainty: Identity Renegotiation among Contingent Workers," *Symbolic Interaction* 28/1: 111–34.

Pager, Devah. 2003. "The Mark of a Criminal Record," *American Journal of Sociology* 108/5: 937–75.

Parkin, Frank. 1979. *Marxism and Class Theory: A Bourgeois Critique*. New York: Columbia University Press.

Paules, Greta Foff. 1991. *Dishing It Out: Power and Resistance among Waitresses in a New Jersey Restaurant*. Philadelphia, PA: Temple University Press.

Penn, R., and Sleightholme D. 1995. "Skilled Work in Contemporary Europe: A Journey into the Dark," in E. Dittrich, G. Schmidt, and R. Whitley, eds, *Industrial Transformation in Europe*. London: Sage, pp. 187–202.

Perlin, Ross. 2011. "Unpaid Interns, Complicit Colleges," *New York Times*, April 3: WK11. Available at: <http://www.nytimes.com/2011/04/03/opinion/03perlin.html>.

Peters, Thomas J., and Robert H. Waterman. 1982. *In Search of Excellence: Lessons from America's Best-Run Companies*. New York: Harper & Row.

Petersen, Trond, Ishak Saporta, and Marc-David L. Seidel. 2000. "Offering a Job: Meritocracy and Social Networks," *American Journal of Sociology* 106/3: 763–816.

Pfeffer, Jeffery, and James Baron. 1988. "Taking the Workers Back Out: Recent Trends in the Structuring of Employment," *Research in Organizational Behavior* 10: 46.

Pink, Daniel H. 2001. *Free Agent Nation: How America's New Independent Workers are Transforming the Way We Live*. New York: Warner Books.

Piore, Michael J., and Charles F. Sabel. 1984. *The Second Industrial Divide: Possibilities for Prosperity*. New York: Basic Books.

Piven, Frances Fox, and Richard A. Cloward. 1977. *Poor People's Movements: Why They Succeed, How They Fail*. New York: Pantheon Books.

Polanyi, Karl. 1944. *The Great Transformation*. Boston, MA: Beacon Press.

Pollert, Anna. 1991. *Farewell to Flexibility?* (Warwick Studies in Industrial Relations). Oxford: Blackwell.

Portes, Alejandro. 1998. "Social Capital: Its Origins and Applications in Modern Sociology," *Annual Review of Sociology* 24: 1–24.

Powell, Walter W. 1990. "Neither Market Nor Hierarchy: Network Forms of Organization," *Research in Organizational Behavior* 12: 42.

Powell, Walter W. 2001. "The Capitalist Firm in the Twenty-First Century: Emerging Patterns in Western Enterprise," in P. DiMaggio, ed., *The Twenty-First Century Firm*. Princeton, NJ: Princeton University Press, pp. 33–68.

Powell, Walter W., Kenneth W. Koput, and Laurel Smith-Doerr. 1996.

"Interorganizational Collaboration and the Locus of Innovation: Networks of Learning in Biotechnology," *Administrative Science Quarterly* 41 (March): 116–45.

Powell, W. W., Douglas R. White, Kenneth W. Koput, and Jason Owen-Smith. 2005. "Network Dynamics and Field Evolution: The Growth of Inter-organizational Collaboration in the Life Sciences," *American Journal of Sociology* 110/4 (January): 1132–1205.

Rama, Martin. 2003. *Globalization and Workers in Developing Countries.* Washington, DC: The World Bank Development Research Group.

Reich, Robert B. 1991. *The Work of Nations: Preparing Ourselves for 21st-century Capitalism.* New York: A.A. Knopf.

Reskin, Barbara F. 2003. "Including Mechanisms in Our Models of Ascriptive Inequality," *American Sociological Review* 68/1: 1–21.

Reskin, Barbara, and Catherine E. Ross. 1992. "Jobs, Authority, and Earnings among Managers: The Continuing Significance of Sex," *Work and Occupations* 19: 342–65.

Reskin, Barbara, and Irene Padavic. 2003. *Women and Men at Work* (Sociology for a New Century). Thousand Oaks, CA: Pine Forge Press.

Reskin, Barbara F., and Roos, Patricia A. 1990. *Job Queues, Gender Queues: Explaining Women's Inroads Into Male Occupations.* Philadelphia, PA: Temple University Press.

Reynolds, Jeremy. 2006. "Teams, Teams, Everywhere? Job and Establishment-Level Predictors of Team Use in the United States," *Social Science Research* 35/1: 252–78.

Rifkin, Jeremy. 2004. *The End of Work.* New York: Putnam.

Rinaldi, A. 2005. "The Emilian Model Revisited: Twenty Years After," *Business History* 47/2: 244–66.

Rodríguez-Garavito, César. 2005. "Global Governance and Labor Rights: Codes of Conduct and Anti-Sweatshop Struggles in Global Apparel Factories in Mexico and Guatemala," *Politics & Society* 33/2: 203–33.

Roethlisberger, F. J., and William J. Dickson. 1939. *Management and the Worker.* Cambridge, MA: Harvard University Press.

Roscigno, Vincent J., Lisette Garcia, and Donna Bobbitt-Zeher. 2007. "Social Closure and Processes of Race/Sex Employment Discrimination," *Annals of the American Academy of Political and Social Sciences* 609: 16–48.

Roscigno, Vincent J., Randy Hodson, and Steven H. Lopez. 2009. "Workplace Incivilities: The Role of Interest Conflicts, Social Closure and Organizational Chaos," *Work Employment Society* 23: 747–72.

Rose, Nikolas S. 1990. *Governing the Soul: The Shaping of the Private Self.* London/New York: Routledge.

Rose, Sonya O. 1992. *Limited Livelihoods: Gender and Class in Nineteenth-Century England*. Berkeley, CA: University of California Press.

Ross, Andrew. 1997. *No Sweat: Fashion, Free Trade and the Rights of Garment Workers*. New York: Verso.

Ross, Andrew. 2008. "The New Geography of Work: Power to the Precarious?," *Theory, Culture & Society* 25/7–8: 31–49.

Ross, Catherine E., and Barbara Reskin. 1992. "Education, Control at Work, and Job Satisfaction," *Social Science Research* 21: 15.

Roy, Donald. 1952. "Quota Restriction and Goldbricking in a Machine Shop," *American Journal of Sociology* 67/2: 427–42.

Roy, Donald 1954. "Efficiency and 'the Fix': Informal Intergroup Relations in a Piecework Machine Shop," *American Journal of Sociology* 60/3: 255–66.

Roy, Donald. 1960. "'Banana Time': Job Satisfaction and Informal Interaction," *Human Organization* 18, 4 (winter): 158–68

Royster, Deirdre A. 2003. *Race and the Invisible Hand: How White Networks Exclude Black Men from Blue-Collar Jobs*. Berkeley, CA: University of California.

Rubin, Beth A. 1995. "Flexible Accumulation: The Decline of Contract and Social Transformation," *Research in Social Stratification and Mobility* 27: 297–323.

Rubin, Beth A. 1996. *Shifts in the Social Contract: Understanding Change in American Society*. Thousand Oaks, CA: Pine Forge.

Rudra, Nita. Fall 2005. "Are Workers in the Developing World 'Winners' or 'Losers' in the Current Era of Globalization?," *Studies in Comparative International Development*. 40/3 (fall): 29–64.

Sabel, Charles F. 1982. *Work and Politics: The Division of Labor in Industry*. Cambridge: Cambridge University Press.

Sabel, Charles, Gary Herrigel, Richard Deeg, and Richard Kazis, 1989. "Regional Prosperities Compared: Massachusetts and Baden-Wurttemberg in the 1980s." *Economy and Society* 18/4: 374–404.

Sallaz, Jeffrey J. 2002. "The House Rules: Autonomy and Interests among Contemporary Casino Croupiers," *Work and Occupations* 29/4: 394–427.

Sallaz, Jeffrey J. 2009. *The Labor of Luck: Casino Capitalism in the United States and South Africa*. Berkeley, CA: University of California Press.

Salzinger, Leslie. 2003. *Genders in Production: Making Workers in Mexico's Global Factories*. Berkeley, CA: University of California Press.

Saxenian, AnnaLee. 1994. *Regional Advantage: Culture and Competition in Silicon Valley and Route 128*. Cambridge, MA: Harvard University Press.

Schrank, Andrew. 2001. "Export Processing Zones: Free Market Islands or Bridges to Structural Transformation?," *Development Policy Review* 19/2: 223–42.

Schrank, Andrew. 2004. "Ready-to-Wear Development? Foreign Investment, Technology Transfer, and Learning-by-Watching in the Apparel Trade," *Social Forces* 83/1: 123–56

Seccombe, Wally, 1986. "Patriarchy Stabilized: The Construction of the Male Breadwinner Norm in 19th Century Britain," *Social History* 2: 45–65.

Seidman, G. W. 2007. *Beyond the Boycott: Labor Rights, Human Rights, and Transnational Activism.* New York: Russell Sage Foundation.

Sennett, Richard. 1998. *The Corrosion of Character: The Personal Consequences of the New Capitalism.* New York: Knopf.

Sewell, Graham. 1995. "How the Giraffe Got Its Neck: An Organization 'Just So' Story," in *Sixth APROS International Colloquium.* Mexico City, Mexico: Metropolitan Autonomous University

Sherman, Rachel. 2007. *Class Acts.* Berkeley, CA: University of California.

Simpson, Ida Harper. 1989. "The Sociology of Work: Where Have the Workers Gone?," *Social Forces* 67/3: 563–81.

Skaggs, Sheryl 2008. "Producing Change or Bagging Opportunity? The Effects of Discrimination Litigation on Women in Supermarket Management," *American Journal of Sociology* 113/4: 1148–82.

Smith, Adam. 1939 [1776]. *The Wealth of Nations: An Inquiry into the Nature and Causes of the Wealth of Nations.* New York: Random House.

Smith, James H., and Jeffrey Mantz. 2006. "Do Cellular Phones Dream of Civil War?: The Mystification of Production and the Consequences of Technology Fetishism in the Eastern Congo," in Max Kirsch, ed., *Inclusion and Exclusion in the Global Arena.* New York: Routledge, pp. 71–94.

Smith, Ryan A. 1997. "Race, Income and Authority at Work: A Cross-Temporal Analysis of Black and White Men," *Social Problems* 44: 19.

Smith, Ryan A. 2001. "Particularism in Control over Monetary Resources at Work: An Analysis of Racio-Ethnic Differences in the Authority Outcomes of Black, White, and Latino Men," *Work and Occupations* 28: 22.

Smith, Ryan A., and James R. Elliott. 2002. "Does Ethnic Concentration Influence Employees' Access to Authority? An Examination of Contemporary Urban Labor Markets," *Social Forces* 81: 25.

Smith, Vicki. 2010. "Enhancing Employability: Human, Cultural, and Social Capital in an Era of Turbulent Unpredictability," *Human Relations* 63/2 (February): 279–300.

Snyder, Karrie Ann, and Adam Isaiah Green. 2008. "Revisiting the Glass Escalator: The Case of Gender Segregation in a Female Dominated Occupation," *Social Problems* 2: 29.

Stark, David. 1980. "Class Struggle and the Transformation of the Labor Process: A Relational Approach," *Theory and Society* 9: 42.

Storper, M. 1994. "The Transition to Flexible Specialization: The Division of Labour, External Economies, and the Crossing of Industrial Divides," in A. Amin, ed., *PostFordism*. Oxford: Blackwell, pp. 195–226.

Strauss, A. 1978. *Negotiations: Varieties, Processes, Contexts, and Social Order*. San Francisco, CA: Jossey-Bass.

Su, Julie. 1997. "El Monte Thai Garment Workers: Slave Sweatshops," in A. Ross, ed., *No Sweat: Fashion, Free Trade, and the Rights of Garment Workers*. New York: Verso, pp. 143–51.

Sutton, John R., Frank Dobbin, John Meyer, and W. Richard Scott. 1994. "The Legalization of the Workplace," *American Journal of Sociology* 99: 944–71.

Tarì, Marcello, and Ilaria Vanni. 2005. "On the Life and Deeds of San Precario, Patron Saint of Precarious Workers and Lives," in *Fibreculture: Internet Theory, Criticism, Research* 5; available at: <http://journal.fibreculture.org/issue5/vanni_tari.html>; accessed June 27, 2010.

Thomas, Robert J. 1994. *What Machines Can't Do: Politics and Technology in the Industrial Enterprise*. Berkeley, CA: University of California Press.

Thompson, Edward Palmer. 1964. *The Making of the English Working Class*. New York: Pantheon Books.

Tienda, Marta, and D. Lii. 1987. "Minority Concentration and Earnings Inequality: Blacks, Hispanics and Asians Compared," *American Journal of Sociology* 93/1 (July): 141–65.

Tomaskovic-Devey, Donald. 1993. *Gender & Racial Inequality at Work: The Sources and Consequences of Job Segregation*. Ithaca, NY: Cornell University School of Industrial and Labor Relations.

Tomaskovic-Devey, Donald, Catherine Zimmer, Kevin Stainback, Corre Robinson, Tiffany Taylor, and Tricia McTague, 2006. "Documenting Desegregation: Segregation in American Workplaces by Race, Ethnicity, and Sex 1966–2000," *American Sociological Review* 71/4: 565–88.

Tomaskovic-Devey, Donald, and Ken-hou Lin. Forthcoming. "Economic Rents and the Financialization of the US Economy," *American Sociological Review*.

Townsend, Anthony, and K. Dow Scott. 2001. "Team Racial Composition, Member Attitudes, and Performance: A Field Study,"

Industrial Relations: A Journal of Economy and Society 40/2 (April): 317–37.

Useem, Michael. 1996. *Investor Capitalism: How Money Managers Are Changing the Face of Corporate America.* New York: Basic Books.

US Glass Ceiling Commission. 1995a. "Good for Business: Making Full Use of the Nation's Human Capital: The Environmental Scan; A Fact-Finding Report of the Federal Glass Ceiling Commission." Washington, DC: US Government Printing Office. Available at: <http://www.dol.gov/oasam/programs/history/reich/reports/ceiling.pdf>; accessed July 4, 2011.

US Glass Ceiling Commission. 1995b. "A Solid Investment: Making Full Use of the Nation's Human Capital (Final Report of the Commission)." Washington, DC: US Government Printing Office. Available at: <http://digitalcommons.ilr.cornell.edu/key_work place/120/>.

Uzzi, Brian. 1997. "Social Structure and Competition in Interfirm Networks: The Paradox of Embeddedness," *Administrative Science Quarterly* 42/1: 35–67.

Vallas, Steven P. 1993. *Power in the Workplace: The Politics of Production at AT&T.* Albany, NY: SUNY.

Vallas, Steven P. 1999. "Rethinking Post-Fordism: The Meanings of Workplace Flexibility," *Sociological Theory* 17/1: 68–101.

Vallas, Steven P. 2001. "Symbolic Boundaries and the Re-Division of Labor: Engineers, Workers, and the Restructuring of Factory Life," *Research in Social Stratification and Mobility* 18: 3–37.

Vallas, Steven P. 2003a. "Why Teamwork Fails: Obstacles to Workplace Change in Four Manufacturing Plants," *American Sociological Review* 68/2: 223–50.

Vallas, Steven P. 2003b. "The 'Knitting of Racial Groups' Revisited: Re-Discovering the Color Line at Work," *Work and Occupations* 30/4 (November): 379–400.

Vallas, Steven P. 2003c. "The Adventures of Managerial Hegemony: Teamwork, Ideology, and Worker Resistance," *Social Problems* 50/2: 204–25.

Vallas, Steven P. 2006. "Empowerment Redux: Structure, Agency, and the Re-Making of Managerial Authority," *American Journal of Sociology* 111/5: 1677–1717.

Vallas, Steven P., and Daniel L. Kleinman. 2008. "Contradiction, Convergence and the Knowledge Economy: The Confluence of Academic and Industrial Biotechnology," *Socio-Economic Review* 6/2: 283–311.

Vallas, S. P., and Andrea Hill. Forthcoming. "Conceptualizing Power in Organizations," *Research in the Sociology of Organizations.*

Warhurst, Chris, and Dennis Nickson. 2007. "Employee Experience of Aesthetic Labour in Retail and Hospitality," *Work, Employment, and Society* 21/1 (March): 18.

Weber, Max, 1978 [1903]. *Economy and Society: An Outline of Interpretive Sociology*, ed. G. Roth and C. Wittich. Berkeley, CA: University of California Press.

Weeks, John. 2004. *Unpopular Culture: The Ritual of Complaint in a British Bank*. Chicago, IL: University of Chicago Press.

Welter, B. 1966. "The Cult of True Womanhood: 1820–1860," *American Quarterly* 18: 24.

Whitford, Josh. 2005. *The New Old Economy: Networks, Institutions, and the Organizational Transformation of American Manufacturing*. Oxford: Oxford University Press.

Whitford, Josh, and Cuz Potter. 2007. "Regional Economies, Open Networks and the Spatial Fragmentation of Production," *Socio-Economic Review* 5: 1–30.

Williams, Christine L.. 1992. "The Glass Escalator: Hidden Advantages for Men in the 'Female' Professions," *Social Problems* 39/3: 253–67.

Williams, Christine L. 1995. *Still a Man's World: Men Who Do Women's Work*. Berkeley, CA: University of California.

Williams, K. Y., and O'Reilly, C. A. 1998. "Demography and Diversity in Organization," in B. M. Straw and R. M. Sutton, eds, *Research in Organizational Behavior* 20. Stamford, CA: JAI Press, pp. 77–140.

Willis, Paul. 1977. *Learning to Labour: How Working Class Kids Get Working Class Jobs*. New York: Columbia University Press.

Willis, Paul. 1979. "Masculinity and Factory Labour," in John Clarke et al., eds., *Working Class Culture*. London: Hutchinson, pp. 185–98.

Willmott, H. 1993. "Strength is Ignorance; Slavery is Freedom: Managing Culture in Modern Organizations," *Journal of Management Studies* 30/4: 515–52.

Wilson, William J. 1996. *When Work Disappears: The World of the New Urban Poor*. New York: Random House.

Wingfield, Adia Harvey. 2009. "Racializing the Glass Escalator: Reconsidering Men's Experiences with Women's Work," *Gender & Society* 23/1: 5–26.

Witz, Anne, Chris Warhurst, and Dennis Nickson. 2003. "The Labour of Aesthetics and the Aesthetics of Organization," *Organization* 10/1: 33–54.

Xiaomin, Yu. 2007. "Transnational Corporation's Code of Conduct and Labor Standards in China's Foreign-Invested Enterprise: A Transnational-National-Local Empirical Study," *Sociological Studies*. Available at: <http://en.cnki.com.cn/Article_en/CJFDTOTAL-SHXJ200705006.htm>.

Zuboff, Shoshana. 1988. *In the Age of the Smart Machine*. New York: Basic Books.

Index